50 Poland Restaurant Dessert Recipes for Home

By: Kelly Johnson

Table of Contents

- Sernik (Polish Cheesecake)
- Paczki (Polish Doughnuts)
- Makowiec (Poppy Seed Roll)
- Babka (Polish Sweet Bread)
- Kremówka (Cream Cake)
- Rogaliki (Polish Crescent Rolls)
- Piernik (Gingerbread)
- Faworki (Angel Wings)
- Żurawinowy Placek (Cranberry Cake)
- Jabłecznik (Apple Cake)
- Zupa Truskawkowa (Strawberry Soup)
- Kluski Śląskie z Jagodami (Silesian Dumplings with Blueberries)
- Leniwe Pierogi (Lazy Pierogi)
- Ciasto Marchewkowe (Carrot Cake)
- Chruściki (Crispy Pastry Twists)
- Ziemniaczane Racuchy (Potato Pancakes)
- Kluski na Parze (Steamed Dumplings)
- Sernik na Zimno (No-Bake Cheesecake)
- Rurki z Kremem (Pastry Tubes with Cream)
- Deser Słodki z Kaszy (Sweet Buckwheat Dessert)
- Racuchy (Apple Pancakes)
- Słodki Kołacz (Sweet Cołacz)
- Ciasto Drożdżowe z Owocami (Yeast Cake with Fruit)
- Babeczki (Cupcakes)
- Tarta z Owocami (Fruit Tart)
- Keks (Fruit Cake)
- Ciasto Puchowe (Fluffy Cake)
- Kisiel (Fruit Jelly)
- Tiramisu (Polish Style)
- Orzechowiec (Nut Cake)
- Czekoladowe Muffinki (Chocolate Muffins)
- Kokosanki (Coconut Macaroons)

- Ciasto Kakaowe (Cocoa Cake)
- Tort Śmietanowy (Cream Cake)
- Ciasto Serowo-Malina (Cheese-Raspberry Cake)
- Mazurek (Easter Cake)
- Sernik Z Owoce (Cheesecake with Fruit)
- Kruszonka (Crumb Topping)
- Kogel Mogel (Egg Yolk Dessert)
- Śliwki w Czekoladzie (Plums in Chocolate)
- Rogaliki Świętomarcińskie (St. Martin's Croissants)
- Tarta Rabarbarowa (Rhubarb Tart)
- Ciasto Malinowe (Raspberry Cake)
- Czernina (Duck Blood Soup with Raisins)
- Placek Z Cynamonem (Cinnamon Cake)
- Ciasto Dyniowe (Pumpkin Cake)
- Zupa Jabłkowa (Apple Soup)
- Pączki z Różą (Rose-filled Doughnuts)
- Kardamonowe Bułeczki (Cardamom Buns)
- Tarta Cytrynowa (Lemon Tart)

Sernik (Polish Cheesecake)

Ingredients:

For the Crust:

- 200g (about 2 cups) graham cracker crumbs or digestive biscuits, crushed
- 100g (about 1/2 cup) unsalted butter, melted
- 2 tablespoons granulated sugar (optional)

For the Filling:

- 1 kg (about 2.2 lbs) farmer's cheese or ricotta cheese (drained)
- 250g (about 1 cup) granulated sugar
- 4 large eggs
- 1 cup sour cream
- 1 teaspoon vanilla extract
- Zest of 1 lemon
- Juice of 1 lemon
- 2 tablespoons all-purpose flour (optional, for thicker texture)

For the Topping (optional):

- Powdered sugar, for dusting
- Fresh fruit or fruit compote

Instructions:

1. **Preheat Oven:** Preheat your oven to 175°C (350°F).
2. **Prepare the Crust:**
   - In a bowl, combine the crushed graham cracker crumbs (or digestive biscuits) with melted butter and sugar (if using).
   - Press the mixture firmly into the bottom of a springform pan (about 9 inches in diameter) to form an even layer.
   - Bake the crust for 10 minutes, then remove from the oven and let it cool slightly.
3. **Prepare the Filling:**
   - In a large mixing bowl, beat the farmer's cheese (or ricotta) with sugar until smooth and creamy.
   - Add the eggs one at a time, beating well after each addition.
   - Mix in the sour cream, vanilla extract, lemon zest, and lemon juice. If you prefer a thicker texture, you can add flour and mix until well combined.
4. **Bake the Cheesecake:**
   - Pour the cheesecake filling over the cooled crust in the springform pan.
   - Smooth the top with a spatula.

- Bake in the preheated oven for about 60-70 minutes, or until the center is set and the top is lightly golden. A toothpick inserted into the center should come out mostly clean.
- Turn off the oven, crack the oven door slightly, and let the cheesecake cool in the oven for about an hour.

5. **Chill the Cheesecake:**
    - After cooling, refrigerate the cheesecake for at least 4 hours, preferably overnight, to fully set and develop its flavors.
6. **Serve:**
    - Before serving, dust with powdered sugar if desired and top with fresh fruit or fruit compote if you like.

Enjoy your delicious Polish cheesecake!

Paczki (Polish Doughnuts)

Ingredients:

For the Dough:

- 500g (about 4 cups) all-purpose flour
- 50g (about 1/4 cup) granulated sugar
- 2 teaspoons active dry yeast
- 1 cup whole milk
- 4 large egg yolks
- 1/2 cup unsalted butter, softened
- 1 teaspoon vanilla extract
- 1/4 teaspoon salt
- Zest of 1 lemon
- 1/4 cup dark rum or brandy (optional, for flavor)

For the Filling:

- 1 cup fruit preserves (e.g., raspberry, apricot) or custard (optional)

For Frying:

- Vegetable oil, for frying

For Coating:

- 1 cup granulated sugar
- Powdered sugar, for dusting (optional)

Instructions:

1. **Prepare the Dough:**
   - In a small saucepan, heat the milk until it's warm (not hot). Sprinkle the yeast over the milk, stir, and let it sit for about 5-10 minutes until foamy.
   - In a large mixing bowl, combine the flour, granulated sugar, and salt. Make a well in the center and add the yeast mixture, egg yolks, butter, vanilla extract, lemon zest, and rum (if using).
   - Mix until a dough forms. Knead the dough on a floured surface for about 8-10 minutes, or until smooth and elastic. You can also use a stand mixer with a dough hook for this process.
   - Place the dough in a greased bowl, cover it with a clean cloth or plastic wrap, and let it rise in a warm place for about 1-2 hours, or until doubled in size.
2. **Shape the Doughnuts:**

- Punch down the dough and transfer it to a floured surface. Roll it out to about 1/2 inch thickness.
- Use a round cutter (about 2-3 inches in diameter) to cut out circles. If you're filling them, use a smaller cutter or glass to cut out a smaller circle in the center of half of the dough circles for filling later.
- Place a small spoonful of fruit preserves or custard in the center of the larger circles. Place a cut-out circle on top and press the edges to seal. You can also leave them plain for filled doughnuts, sealing the edges tightly.

3. **Fry the Doughnuts:**
   - Heat about 2 inches of vegetable oil in a large, deep skillet or fryer to 180°C (350°F).
   - Fry the doughnuts in batches, being careful not to overcrowd the pan. Cook each side for about 2-3 minutes, or until golden brown and cooked through.
   - Remove the doughnuts with a slotted spoon and drain them on paper towels.

4. **Coat the Doughnuts:**
   - While the doughnuts are still warm, roll them in granulated sugar to coat. If desired, dust with powdered sugar after cooling slightly.

5. **Serve:**
   - Enjoy your fresh, homemade pączki warm or at room temperature. They are best enjoyed on the day they are made but can be stored in an airtight container for a couple of days.

Note: For a traditional filling, you can also use jam or sweetened cream cheese. If you want to inject the filling after frying, use a piping bag fitted with a nozzle.

Enjoy your delicious, homemade Polish doughnuts!

Makowiec (Poppy Seed Roll)

Ingredients:

For the Dough:

- 500g (about 4 cups) all-purpose flour
- 100g (about 1/2 cup) granulated sugar
- 10g (about 2 teaspoons) active dry yeast
- 200ml (about 3/4 cup + 2 tablespoons) whole milk
- 2 large egg yolks
- 100g (about 1/2 cup) unsalted butter, softened
- 1 teaspoon vanilla extract
- 1/4 teaspoon salt

For the Poppy Seed Filling:

- 250g (about 2 cups) poppy seeds
- 200g (about 1 cup) granulated sugar
- 50g (about 1/4 cup) unsalted butter
- 200ml (about 3/4 cup) milk
- 1/2 cup honey
- 1/2 teaspoon vanilla extract
- 100g (about 1 cup) raisins or currants (optional)
- Zest of 1 lemon
- 1/2 teaspoon ground cinnamon

For the Glaze:

- 1 egg, beaten
- Powdered sugar, for dusting (optional)

Instructions:

1. **Prepare the Dough:**
    - In a small saucepan, warm the milk until it's lukewarm (not hot). Sprinkle the yeast over the milk, stir, and let it sit for about 5-10 minutes until foamy.
    - In a large mixing bowl, combine the flour, sugar, and salt. Make a well in the center and add the yeast mixture, egg yolks, butter, and vanilla extract.
    - Mix until a dough forms. Knead the dough on a floured surface for about 8-10 minutes, or until smooth and elastic. Alternatively, use a stand mixer with a dough hook.
    - Place the dough in a greased bowl, cover with a clean cloth or plastic wrap, and let it rise in a warm place for about 1-2 hours, or until doubled in size.
2. **Prepare the Poppy Seed Filling:**
    - Place the poppy seeds in a bowl and pour boiling water over them. Let them sit for about 10 minutes, then drain and grind the poppy seeds in a food processor or coffee grinder until fine.

- In a saucepan, combine the milk, butter, honey, and vanilla extract. Heat until the butter is melted and the mixture is warm. Stir in the ground poppy seeds and sugar. Cook over low heat for about 5-10 minutes, stirring frequently, until thickened.
- Remove from heat and let it cool slightly. Stir in the raisins (if using), lemon zest, and cinnamon.

3. **Assemble the Roll:**
    - Preheat your oven to 180°C (350°F).
    - Punch down the dough and transfer it to a floured surface. Roll it out into a rectangle about 1/4 inch thick.
    - Spread the poppy seed filling evenly over the dough, leaving a small border around the edges.
    - Carefully roll the dough into a tight log, sealing the edges and the seam.
    - Place the rolled dough seam-side down on a parchment-lined baking sheet.

4. **Bake the Roll:**
    - Brush the top of the roll with the beaten egg to give it a nice golden color.
    - Bake in the preheated oven for about 35-45 minutes, or until the roll is golden brown and sounds hollow when tapped.
    - Let the roll cool on a wire rack.

5. **Serve:**
    - Once cooled, dust with powdered sugar if desired. Slice and enjoy!

Makowiec is delicious on its own, but it also pairs wonderfully with a cup of tea or coffee. Enjoy this traditional Polish treat!

Babka (Polish Sweet Bread)

Ingredients:

For the Dough:

- 500g (about 4 cups) all-purpose flour
- 100g (about 1/2 cup) granulated sugar
- 10g (about 2 teaspoons) active dry yeast
- 200ml (about 3/4 cup + 2 tablespoons) whole milk
- 4 large egg yolks
- 100g (about 1/2 cup) unsalted butter, softened
- 1 teaspoon vanilla extract
- 1/4 teaspoon salt
- Zest of 1 lemon

For the Filling:

- 200g (about 1 cup) granulated sugar
- 100g (about 1/2 cup) unsalted butter, melted
- 1 tablespoon ground cinnamon
- 1 cup chopped nuts (e.g., walnuts, almonds) or raisins (optional)
- 1/2 cup cocoa powder (optional, for a chocolate version)

For the Glaze:

- 1 cup powdered sugar
- 2-3 tablespoons milk or lemon juice

Instructions:

1. **Prepare the Dough:**
    - In a small saucepan, warm the milk until it's lukewarm (not hot). Sprinkle the yeast over the milk, stir, and let it sit for about 5-10 minutes until foamy.
    - In a large mixing bowl, combine the flour, sugar, and salt. Make a well in the center and add the yeast mixture, egg yolks, butter, vanilla extract, and lemon zest.
    - Mix until a dough forms. Knead the dough on a floured surface for about 8-10 minutes, or until smooth and elastic. Alternatively, use a stand mixer with a dough hook.
    - Place the dough in a greased bowl, cover it with a clean cloth or plastic wrap, and let it rise in a warm place for about 1-2 hours, or until doubled in size.
2. **Prepare the Filling:**

- In a bowl, mix together the granulated sugar, melted butter, and ground cinnamon. If you're making a chocolate babka, you can also mix in cocoa powder.
- If using nuts or raisins, chop them and add them to the filling mixture.

3. **Assemble the Babka:**
   - Punch down the dough and transfer it to a floured surface. Roll it out into a large rectangle (about 1/4 inch thick).
   - Spread the filling evenly over the dough, leaving a small border around the edges.
   - Roll the dough tightly into a log, then slice the log lengthwise to expose the filling. Twist the two halves together to form a spiral shape.
   - Place the twisted dough into a greased bundt pan or two greased loaf pans.

4. **Second Rise:**
   - Cover the pan(s) with a clean cloth and let the babka rise in a warm place for about 30-45 minutes, or until puffy.

5. **Bake the Babka:**
   - Preheat your oven to 180°C (350°F).
   - Bake in the preheated oven for about 35-45 minutes, or until the babka is golden brown and a skewer inserted into the center comes out clean.
   - Allow the babka to cool in the pan for about 10 minutes, then transfer it to a wire rack to cool completely.

6. **Glaze the Babka:**
   - While the babka is cooling, make the glaze by mixing powdered sugar with milk or lemon juice until smooth.
   - Drizzle the glaze over the cooled babka.

Serve:

- Enjoy the babka sliced with coffee or tea. It's best fresh but can be stored in an airtight container for a few days.

This sweet bread is wonderfully versatile and can be customized with different fillings and toppings. Enjoy baking and indulging in this traditional Polish treat!

Krémówka (Cream Cake)

Ingredients:

For the Pastry:

- 2 sheets of puff pastry (store-bought or homemade), thawed if frozen

For the Cream Filling:

- 500ml (about 2 cups) whole milk
- 1 vanilla bean or 2 teaspoons vanilla extract
- 4 large egg yolks
- 100g (about 1/2 cup) granulated sugar
- 40g (about 1/4 cup) cornstarch
- 100g (about 1/2 cup) unsalted butter, softened
- 200ml (about 3/4 cup) heavy cream

For Dusting:

- Powdered sugar

Instructions:

1. **Prepare the Pastry:**
   - Preheat your oven to 200°C (400°F).
   - Place the puff pastry sheets on a parchment-lined baking sheet. Prick the surface of the pastry with a fork to prevent it from puffing up too much.
   - Bake in the preheated oven for about 15-20 minutes, or until golden and crispy.
   - Remove from the oven and let it cool completely. Once cooled, carefully trim any uneven edges to create neat rectangles.
2. **Prepare the Cream Filling:**
   - In a saucepan, heat the milk and vanilla bean (if using) until just before boiling. If using vanilla extract, add it later.
   - In a mixing bowl, whisk together the egg yolks, granulated sugar, and cornstarch until smooth.
   - Gradually whisk in the hot milk mixture into the egg yolk mixture to temper the eggs.
   - Return the mixture to the saucepan and cook over medium heat, whisking constantly, until it thickens and comes to a boil. This should take about 5-7 minutes.
   - Remove from heat and stir in the vanilla extract if you didn't use a vanilla bean. Let the custard cool slightly.
   - Once the custard has cooled to room temperature, beat the softened butter until creamy and then gradually beat in the custard until smooth and well combined.

- In a separate bowl, whip the heavy cream until stiff peaks form. Gently fold the whipped cream into the custard mixture.
3. **Assemble the Kremówka:**
   - Place one sheet of puff pastry on a serving platter.
   - Spread the cream filling evenly over the pastry layer.
   - Top with the second sheet of puff pastry, pressing down gently to adhere.
   - Refrigerate for at least 2 hours to allow the cream to set and the flavors to meld.
4. **Serve:**
   - Before serving, dust the top of the Kremówka with powdered sugar.
   - Slice and enjoy this elegant and delicious Polish cream cake!

Tips:

- You can make the custard and whipped cream ahead of time, but assemble the cake just before serving to keep the puff pastry crisp.
- For a more traditional touch, you can sprinkle additional powdered sugar on top just before serving.

Enjoy your delightful Kremówka, a true Polish classic!

Rogaliki (Polish Crescent Rolls)

Ingredients:

For the Dough:

- 500g (about 4 cups) all-purpose flour
- 250g (about 1 cup) unsalted butter, chilled and cubed
- 100g (about 1/2 cup) granulated sugar
- 1/2 teaspoon salt
- 2 large egg yolks
- 200ml (about 3/4 cup) sour cream
- 1 teaspoon vanilla extract (optional)

For the Filling:

- 200g (about 1 cup) fruit preserves (e.g., apricot, raspberry, or strawberry)
- 100g (about 1 cup) finely chopped nuts (optional)
- 1 tablespoon granulated sugar (for mixing with the nuts, optional)

For Coating:

- 1 egg, beaten (for egg wash)
- Powdered sugar (for dusting, optional)

Instructions:

1. **Prepare the Dough:**
   - In a large bowl, combine the flour, sugar, and salt. Add the chilled butter and mix with your fingers or a pastry cutter until the mixture resembles coarse crumbs.
   - Add the egg yolks, sour cream, and vanilla extract (if using). Mix until the dough comes together.
   - Transfer the dough to a lightly floured surface and knead gently until smooth. Divide the dough into 2 equal portions, wrap them in plastic wrap, and refrigerate for at least 30 minutes.
2. **Prepare the Filling:**
   - If using nuts, mix them with the granulated sugar.
   - Prepare the fruit preserves by heating them slightly to make them easier to spread, if needed.
3. **Shape the Rogaliki:**
   - Preheat your oven to 180°C (350°F) and line a baking sheet with parchment paper.
   - On a lightly floured surface, roll out one portion of the dough into a circle about 1/8 inch thick.
   - Cut the circle into 8-12 wedges (like slicing a pizza).
   - Place a small spoonful of fruit preserves and/or a sprinkle of nuts at the wide end of each wedge.

- - Roll each wedge from the wide end to the pointed end, forming a crescent shape. Place each rolled crescent on the prepared baking sheet.
4. **Bake the Rogaliki:**
    - Brush the tops of the crescents with the beaten egg to give them a golden finish.
    - Bake in the preheated oven for about 15-20 minutes, or until golden brown and baked through.
5. **Finish and Serve:**
    - Remove the Rogaliki from the oven and let them cool slightly on a wire rack.
    - Dust with powdered sugar before serving, if desired.

Tips:

- For a richer flavor, you can add a touch of cinnamon to the filling.
- Make sure the butter is well-chilled when making the dough to ensure a flaky texture.
- If you want to freeze these rolls, you can freeze them after shaping but before baking. Bake from frozen, adding a few extra minutes to the baking time.

Enjoy your homemade Rogaliki! They're perfect with tea or coffee and make a delightful treat for any time of the day.

Piernik (Gingerbread)

Ingredients:

For the Dough:

- 500g (about 4 cups) all-purpose flour
- 250g (about 1 1/4 cups) honey
- 200g (about 1 cup) granulated sugar
- 100g (about 1/2 cup) unsalted butter
- 1 large egg
- 2 teaspoons ground ginger
- 2 teaspoons ground cinnamon
- 1/2 teaspoon ground cloves
- 1/2 teaspoon ground nutmeg
- 1 teaspoon baking soda
- 1/4 teaspoon salt

For the Glaze (optional):

- 1 cup powdered sugar
- 2-3 tablespoons milk or lemon juice

For Decoration (optional):

- Candied fruit
- Nuts
- Sprinkles

Instructions:

1. **Prepare the Dough:**
   - In a saucepan, gently heat the honey, sugar, and butter until the sugar is dissolved and the mixture is smooth. Remove from heat and let it cool slightly.
   - In a large bowl, whisk together the flour, baking soda, salt, and all the spices (ginger, cinnamon, cloves, and nutmeg).
   - Pour the honey mixture into the flour mixture. Add the egg and mix until a dough forms.
   - Knead the dough on a floured surface until smooth. If the dough is too sticky, you can add a bit more flour.
2. **Chill the Dough:**
   - Wrap the dough in plastic wrap and refrigerate for at least 2 hours, or overnight. Chilling helps the dough to firm up and makes it easier to roll out.
3. **Roll and Cut the Dough:**

- Preheat your oven to 180°C (350°F) and line baking sheets with parchment paper.
- On a floured surface, roll out the dough to about 1/4 inch thickness.
- Use cookie cutters to cut out shapes or use a knife to cut into squares or rectangles. Place the cookies on the prepared baking sheets.
- If you want to decorate with candied fruit or nuts, press them into the top of the cookies before baking.

4. **Bake the Gingerbread:**
   - Bake in the preheated oven for about 10-15 minutes, or until the edges are lightly golden. The baking time can vary depending on the size and thickness of your cookies.
   - Remove from the oven and let the cookies cool on a wire rack.

5. **Glaze and Decorate (optional):**
   - If using a glaze, mix powdered sugar with milk or lemon juice until smooth. Drizzle over the cooled gingerbread cookies.
   - Add any additional decorations like sprinkles or extra nuts while the glaze is still wet.

6. **Store:**
   - Store the gingerbread cookies in an airtight container at room temperature. They will keep well for about 1-2 weeks.

Tips:

- For a softer gingerbread, you can reduce the baking time slightly.
- You can also add a bit of orange or lemon zest to the dough for a citrusy twist.
- Piernik can also be made as a cake rather than cookies. Simply pour the dough into a greased and floured cake pan and bake for about 40-50 minutes, or until a toothpick inserted into the center comes out clean.

Enjoy your delicious, homemade Piernik! It's a festive treat that's sure to be a hit with family and friends.

Faworki (Angel Wings)

Ingredients:

- 2 cups all-purpose flour
- 2 large egg yolks
- 1 whole egg
- 1/2 cup sour cream
- 2 tablespoons granulated sugar
- 1/4 teaspoon salt
- 2 tablespoons unsalted butter, melted
- 1 teaspoon vanilla extract (optional)
- Vegetable oil, for frying
- Powdered sugar, for dusting

Instructions:

1. **Prepare the Dough:**
    - In a large bowl, whisk together the flour, sugar, and salt.
    - Make a well in the center and add the egg yolks, whole egg, sour cream, melted butter, and vanilla extract (if using).
    - Mix until a dough forms. Turn it out onto a floured surface and knead for about 5 minutes, until smooth and elastic.
    - Wrap the dough in plastic wrap and let it rest for at least 30 minutes at room temperature.
2. **Roll and Shape the Dough:**
    - After resting, divide the dough into 2-4 portions. On a floured surface, roll out one portion at a time into a thin rectangle, about 1/8 inch thick.
    - Using a sharp knife or a pizza cutter, cut the dough into strips about 1 inch wide and 3-4 inches long.
    - Make a small cut in the center of each strip. Fold one end of the strip through the cut to form a twist or bow shape. Alternatively, you can shape them into simple twists.
3. **Fry the Faworki:**
    - Heat vegetable oil in a deep skillet or saucepan to 350°F (175°C). You need enough oil to submerge the faworki.
    - Fry the faworki in batches, being careful not to overcrowd the pan. Fry them for about 1-2 minutes per side, or until golden brown and crispy.
    - Use a slotted spoon to transfer the fried faworki to a paper towel-lined plate to drain excess oil.
4. **Dust and Serve:**
    - Once cooled, dust the faworki generously with powdered sugar.
    - Serve and enjoy! These pastries are best enjoyed fresh but can be stored in an airtight container for a few days.

Tips:

- Make sure the oil temperature is correct; if it's too hot, the faworki will burn, and if it's too cold, they will be greasy.
- You can also experiment with adding a bit of zest from an orange or lemon to the dough for extra flavor.

Enjoy these crispy, delicate treats that are perfect for sharing with friends and family!

Żurawinowy Placek (Cranberry Cake)

Ingredients:

For the Cake:

- 200g (about 1 1/2 cups) all-purpose flour
- 150g (about 3/4 cup) granulated sugar
- 1/2 cup unsalted butter, softened
- 2 large eggs
- 1/2 cup sour cream or plain yogurt
- 1 teaspoon vanilla extract
- 1 teaspoon baking powder
- 1/2 teaspoon baking soda
- 1/4 teaspoon salt
- 1 1/2 cups fresh or frozen cranberries (if using frozen, do not thaw)

For the Topping (optional):

- 1/4 cup granulated sugar
- 1/2 teaspoon ground cinnamon

For the Glaze (optional):

- 1/2 cup powdered sugar
- 2-3 tablespoons orange juice or milk

Instructions:

1. **Preheat Oven:**
    - Preheat your oven to 180°C (350°F). Grease and flour a 9-inch round or square cake pan, or line it with parchment paper.
2. **Prepare the Batter:**
    - In a medium bowl, whisk together the flour, baking powder, baking soda, and salt.
    - In a large bowl, beat the softened butter and sugar together until creamy.
    - Add the eggs one at a time, beating well after each addition.
    - Mix in the vanilla extract.
    - Alternately add the flour mixture and sour cream (or yogurt) to the butter mixture, beginning and ending with the flour mixture. Mix until just combined.
    - Gently fold in the cranberries.
3. **Bake the Cake:**
    - Pour the batter into the prepared cake pan and smooth the top.
    - If using, mix the granulated sugar and ground cinnamon together and sprinkle it evenly over the top of the batter.
    - Bake in the preheated oven for about 40-50 minutes, or until a toothpick inserted into the center comes out clean.
4. **Cool and Glaze (optional):**

- Allow the cake to cool in the pan for about 10 minutes, then transfer it to a wire rack to cool completely.
- If you're using the glaze, whisk together the powdered sugar and orange juice (or milk) until smooth. Drizzle over the cooled cake.

5. **Serve:**
   - Slice and serve. This cake pairs wonderfully with a cup of tea or coffee.

Tips:

- If you prefer a less tart cake, you can coat the cranberries with a little flour before folding them into the batter. This helps to distribute them more evenly and prevent them from sinking.
- You can also add a handful of chopped nuts or white chocolate chips to the batter for added texture and flavor.

Enjoy your Żurawinowy Placek! This cranberry cake is a delightful treat with a perfect balance of sweetness and tartness.

Jabłecznik (Apple Cake)

Ingredients:

For the Cake:

- 4 large apples (e.g., Granny Smith or another tart variety), peeled, cored, and thinly sliced
- 200g (about 1 cup) granulated sugar
- 200g (about 1 1/2 cups) all-purpose flour
- 100g (about 1/2 cup) unsalted butter, softened
- 2 large eggs
- 1/2 cup sour cream or plain yogurt
- 1 teaspoon vanilla extract
- 1 teaspoon baking powder
- 1/2 teaspoon baking soda
- 1/4 teaspoon salt
- 1 teaspoon ground cinnamon
- 1/4 teaspoon ground nutmeg (optional)

For the Topping (optional):

- 2 tablespoons granulated sugar
- 1 teaspoon ground cinnamon

For the Glaze (optional):

- 1/2 cup powdered sugar
- 2-3 tablespoons milk or lemon juice

Instructions:

1. **Preheat Oven:**
    - Preheat your oven to 180°C (350°F). Grease and flour a 9-inch round or square cake pan, or line it with parchment paper.
2. **Prepare the Apples:**
    - In a bowl, toss the sliced apples with 1 tablespoon of granulated sugar and 1 teaspoon of ground cinnamon. Set aside.
3. **Prepare the Cake Batter:**
    - In a large bowl, cream together the softened butter and 200g (about 1 cup) of granulated sugar until light and fluffy.
    - Beat in the eggs one at a time, followed by the vanilla extract.
    - In a separate bowl, whisk together the flour, baking powder, baking soda, salt, and nutmeg (if using).
    - Gradually add the dry ingredients to the butter mixture, alternating with the sour cream (or yogurt), beginning and ending with the dry ingredients. Mix until just combined.
4. **Assemble the Cake:**

- Gently fold half of the apple slices into the batter.
- Pour the batter into the prepared cake pan and spread it evenly.
- Arrange the remaining apple slices on top of the batter in a decorative pattern.

5. **Add Topping (optional):**
   - If desired, mix the granulated sugar and ground cinnamon together and sprinkle it over the top of the cake.

6. **Bake the Cake:**
   - Bake in the preheated oven for about 40-50 minutes, or until a toothpick inserted into the center comes out clean and the cake is golden brown.

7. **Cool and Glaze (optional):**
   - Allow the cake to cool in the pan for about 10 minutes, then transfer it to a wire rack to cool completely.
   - If using the glaze, whisk together the powdered sugar and milk (or lemon juice) until smooth. Drizzle over the cooled cake.

8. **Serve:**
   - Slice and serve. This cake is delicious on its own or with a dollop of whipped cream or a scoop of vanilla ice cream.

Tips:

- For extra flavor, you can add a handful of chopped nuts or raisins to the batter.
- If you prefer a less sweet cake, you can reduce the amount of sugar in the recipe or use a tart variety of apples.

Enjoy your Jabłecznik! This apple cake is a comforting and flavorful treat that showcases the wonderful taste of apples.

Zupa Truskawkowa (Strawberry Soup)

Ingredients:

- 500g (about 4 cups) fresh strawberries, hulled and halved
- 750ml (about 3 cups) water or fruit juice (such as apple or orange juice)
- 100g (about 1/2 cup) granulated sugar (adjust to taste)
- 1 tablespoon lemon juice
- 1 teaspoon vanilla extract (optional)
- 2 tablespoons cornstarch
- 2 tablespoons cold water (for cornstarch slurry)
- Fresh mint leaves (for garnish, optional)
- Whipped cream or sour cream (for serving, optional)

Instructions:

1. **Prepare the Strawberries:**
   - In a large pot, combine the strawberries, water or fruit juice, and sugar.
   - Bring to a boil over medium heat, stirring occasionally.
   - Once the mixture reaches a boil, reduce the heat and let it simmer for about 5-10 minutes, or until the strawberries are tender.
2. **Blend the Soup:**
   - Use an immersion blender to puree the soup directly in the pot until smooth. If you don't have an immersion blender, you can carefully transfer the mixture to a regular blender in batches and blend until smooth.
   - Return the soup to the pot if using a regular blender.
3. **Thicken the Soup (optional):**
   - In a small bowl, mix the cornstarch with 2 tablespoons of cold water to create a slurry.
   - Stir the slurry into the soup.
   - Continue to cook over medium heat, stirring constantly, until the soup thickens slightly. This should take about 2-3 minutes.
4. **Add Flavorings:**
   - Stir in the lemon juice and vanilla extract (if using).
   - Taste and adjust the sweetness if needed.
5. **Chill the Soup:**
   - Allow the soup to cool to room temperature, then refrigerate it for at least 2 hours, or until well chilled.
6. **Serve:**
   - Serve the soup chilled, garnished with fresh mint leaves if desired.
   - Optionally, you can add a dollop of whipped cream or a spoonful of sour cream to each serving for extra richness.

Tips:

- For a slightly different flavor, you can add a splash of balsamic vinegar or a few chopped fresh basil leaves to the soup.

- If you prefer a chunkier soup, you can reserve some of the strawberries before blending and add them back in after pureeing.

Enjoy your refreshing Zupa Truskawkowa! This unique strawberry soup is a wonderful way to enjoy the fresh taste of strawberries in a light and satisfying dish.

Kluski Śląskie z Jagodami (Silesian Dumplings with Blueberries)

Ingredients:

For the Dumplings:

- 1 kg (about 2.2 lbs) potatoes, peeled and cubed
- 250g (about 1 1/2 cups) potato flour (also known as potato starch)
- 1 egg
- Salt, to taste

For the Blueberry Sauce:

- 300g (about 2 cups) fresh or frozen blueberries
- 1/4 cup granulated sugar (adjust to taste)
- 1 tablespoon lemon juice
- 1 tablespoon cornstarch (optional, for thickening)
- 2 tablespoons cold water (optional, for cornstarch slurry)

Instructions:

1. **Prepare the Dumplings:**
    - Boil the peeled and cubed potatoes in salted water until tender, about 15-20 minutes. Drain well and let them cool slightly.
    - Mash the potatoes thoroughly or pass them through a potato ricer for a smooth texture.
    - While the potatoes are still warm, add the potato flour, egg, and a pinch of salt. Mix until a smooth dough forms. The dough should be slightly sticky but manageable.
    - Form the dough into small balls, about 1 to 1.5 inches in diameter. Use your thumb or a spoon to make a small indentation in the center of each ball.
2. **Cook the Dumplings:**
    - Bring a large pot of salted water to a boil.
    - Gently drop the dumplings into the boiling water, being careful not to overcrowd the pot. Cook in batches if necessary.
    - When the dumplings float to the surface, continue to cook them for an additional 3-4 minutes, then remove them with a slotted spoon and place them on a plate.
3. **Prepare the Blueberry Sauce:**
    - In a saucepan, combine the blueberries, sugar, and lemon juice.
    - Cook over medium heat, stirring occasionally, until the blueberries release their juices and the sauce begins to thicken, about 5-10 minutes.
    - If you prefer a thicker sauce, mix the cornstarch with the cold water to create a slurry and stir it into the blueberry mixture. Cook for an additional 1-2 minutes until thickened.
4. **Serve:**
    - Serve the warm dumplings topped with the blueberry sauce. You can garnish with a sprinkle of powdered sugar if desired.

Tips:

- You can also use other berries or fruits for the sauce, such as raspberries, strawberries, or cherries.
- If you prefer a richer sauce, you can add a splash of cream or a pat of butter to the blueberry mixture.

Enjoy your **Kluski Śląskie z Jagodami**! These dumplings with blueberries make for a delightful and comforting dish, blending the savory and sweet in a truly satisfying way.

Leniwe Pierogi (Lazy Pierogi)

Ingredients:

For the Dough:

- 500g (about 2 cups) quark or farmer's cheese (you can substitute with ricotta or cottage cheese, but drain any excess liquid)
- 200g (about 1 1/2 cups) all-purpose flour, plus extra for dusting
- 1 large egg
- 1/4 teaspoon salt
- 1/4 teaspoon baking powder

For Cooking and Serving:

- 2-3 tablespoons butter
- 1 large onion, finely chopped
- Salt and pepper, to taste
- Chopped fresh dill or parsley, for garnish (optional)
- Sour cream, for serving (optional)

Instructions:

1. **Prepare the Dough:**
    - In a large bowl, combine the quark (or cheese), flour, egg, salt, and baking powder.
    - Mix until a soft, slightly sticky dough forms. If the dough is too sticky, add a little more flour, a tablespoon at a time.
    - Lightly flour a clean surface and roll out the dough to about 1/2 inch thick.
2. **Cut and Cook the Dough:**
    - Using a knife or a pizza cutter, cut the dough into small squares or rectangles, about 1 inch in size.
    - Bring a large pot of salted water to a boil.
    - Drop the dough squares into the boiling water, being careful not to overcrowd the pot. Cook in batches if necessary.
    - When the dumplings float to the surface, cook for an additional 2-3 minutes until they are cooked through. Remove with a slotted spoon and place on a plate.
3. **Prepare the Topping:**
    - In a large skillet, melt the butter over medium heat.
    - Add the chopped onion and cook until golden brown and caramelized, about 8-10 minutes.
    - Season with salt and pepper.
4. **Serve:**
    - Toss the cooked dumplings in the skillet with the caramelized onions and butter.

- Garnish with chopped fresh dill or parsley, if desired.
- Serve with a dollop of sour cream, if you like.

Tips:

- You can add cooked bacon or ham to the skillet for extra flavor.
- For a different variation, you can mix herbs (like chives or parsley) into the dough for added flavor.

Enjoy your **Leniwe Pierogi**! This dish offers all the flavors of traditional pierogi with much less effort, making it a perfect choice for a quick and satisfying meal.

Ciasto Marchewkowe (Carrot Cake)

Ingredients:

For the Cake:

- 2 cups (about 250g) all-purpose flour
- 1 1/2 teaspoons baking powder
- 1/2 teaspoon baking soda
- 1/2 teaspoon salt
- 1 1/2 teaspoons ground cinnamon
- 1/2 teaspoon ground nutmeg
- 1/2 teaspoon ground ginger
- 1/2 cup (about 100g) granulated sugar
- 1/2 cup (about 100g) packed brown sugar
- 1 cup (about 240ml) vegetable oil
- 4 large eggs
- 2 cups (about 250g) finely grated carrots (about 4 medium carrots)
- 1/2 cup (about 50g) chopped walnuts or pecans (optional)
- 1/2 cup (about 80g) raisins or sultanas (optional)
- 1 teaspoon vanilla extract

For the Cream Cheese Frosting:

- 8 oz (about 225g) cream cheese, softened
- 1/2 cup (about 115g) unsalted butter, softened
- 2-3 cups (about 240-360g) powdered sugar, sifted
- 1 teaspoon vanilla extract

For Decoration (optional):

- Additional chopped nuts
- Shredded coconut
- Carrot decorations

Instructions:

1. **Prepare the Cake Batter:**
    - Preheat your oven to 180°C (350°F). Grease and flour two 9-inch round cake pans, or line them with parchment paper.
    - In a medium bowl, whisk together the flour, baking powder, baking soda, salt, cinnamon, nutmeg, and ginger.
    - In a large bowl, beat together the granulated sugar, brown sugar, and vegetable oil until well combined.
    - Add the eggs one at a time, beating well after each addition.

- Stir in the grated carrots, walnuts (if using), raisins (if using), and vanilla extract.
- Gradually add the dry ingredients to the wet ingredients, mixing until just combined.

2. **Bake the Cake:**
    - Divide the batter evenly between the prepared cake pans.
    - Bake in the preheated oven for about 30-35 minutes, or until a toothpick inserted into the center of the cakes comes out clean.
    - Allow the cakes to cool in the pans for about 10 minutes, then transfer them to a wire rack to cool completely.
3. **Prepare the Cream Cheese Frosting:**
    - In a large bowl, beat together the softened cream cheese and butter until smooth and creamy.
    - Gradually add the powdered sugar, beating until the frosting reaches your desired consistency and sweetness.
    - Stir in the vanilla extract.
4. **Frost the Cake:**
    - Once the cakes are completely cooled, spread a layer of cream cheese frosting on top of one of the cakes.
    - Place the second cake on top and frost the top and sides of the cake with the remaining cream cheese frosting.
    - Decorate with additional chopped nuts, shredded coconut, or carrot decorations if desired.
5. **Serve:**
    - Slice and enjoy! The cake can be stored in the refrigerator for up to 5 days.

Tips:

- Make sure the carrots are finely grated for a smooth texture in the cake.
- You can also add a handful of crushed pineapple (drained) to the batter for extra moisture and flavor.
- For a spiced-up version, consider adding a pinch of allspice or clove to the spice mix.

Enjoy your **Ciasto Marchewkowe**! This classic carrot cake is a delicious treat that's sure to impress and satisfy.

Chruściki (Crispy Pastry Twists)

Ingredients:

- 2 cups all-purpose flour
- 1/4 cup granulated sugar
- 1/2 teaspoon salt
- 1/2 teaspoon baking powder
- 3 large egg yolks
- 1 large egg
- 1/2 cup sour cream or heavy cream
- 2 tablespoons unsalted butter, melted
- 1 teaspoon vanilla extract (optional)
- Vegetable oil, for frying
- Powdered sugar, for dusting

Instructions:

1. **Prepare the Dough:**
   - In a large bowl, whisk together the flour, sugar, salt, and baking powder.
   - Make a well in the center and add the egg yolks, whole egg, sour cream (or heavy cream), melted butter, and vanilla extract (if using).
   - Mix until a dough forms. Turn the dough out onto a floured surface and knead gently until smooth. If the dough is too sticky, add a little more flour as needed.
2. **Roll and Shape the Dough:**
   - Divide the dough into 2-3 portions. On a floured surface, roll out one portion of the dough to about 1/8 inch thick.
   - Use a sharp knife or pizza cutter to cut the dough into strips about 1 inch wide and 4 inches long.
   - Make a small slit in the center of each strip and twist the ends through the slit to form a knot or bow shape. Alternatively, you can just twist the strips into simple spirals or bows.
3. **Fry the Pastries:**
   - In a deep skillet or saucepan, heat the vegetable oil to 350°F (175°C). You need enough oil to submerge the pastries.
   - Fry the pastries in batches, being careful not to overcrowd the pan. Fry for about 1-2 minutes per side, or until golden brown and crispy.
   - Use a slotted spoon to transfer the fried pastries to a paper towel-lined plate to drain excess oil.
4. **Dust with Powdered Sugar:**
   - Once the pastries are cool enough to handle, dust them generously with powdered sugar.
5. **Serve:**

- Serve the Chruściki as a crispy treat with tea or coffee. They are best enjoyed fresh but can be stored in an airtight container for a few days.

Tips:

- Ensure the oil temperature is correct; too hot, and the pastries will burn, too cool, and they will absorb excess oil.
- If you don't have a deep fryer, you can use a deep skillet, but make sure to keep an eye on the oil temperature with a thermometer.

Enjoy your **Chruściki**! These crispy, delicate pastries are sure to be a hit with anyone who tries them.

Ziemniaczane Racuchy (Potato Pancakes)

Ingredients:

- 4 medium potatoes (about 1 lb or 450g)
- 1 small onion, finely grated
- 2 large eggs
- 1/4 cup all-purpose flour (plus extra if needed)
- 1/4 cup potato flour (optional, for extra crispiness)
- 1 teaspoon baking powder
- Salt and pepper, to taste
- 2 tablespoons vegetable oil (for frying)
- Fresh chives or parsley, chopped (for garnish, optional)

Instructions:

1. **Prepare the Potatoes:**
   - Peel and grate the potatoes using a coarse grater or a food processor. You want the potato shreds to be small but not overly fine.
   - Place the grated potatoes in a clean kitchen towel or cheesecloth and squeeze out as much moisture as possible. This step is crucial to get crispy pancakes.
2. **Mix the Batter:**
   - In a large bowl, combine the grated potatoes, finely grated onion, and eggs.
   - Add the flour, potato flour (if using), baking powder, salt, and pepper. Mix until well combined. The batter should be thick but spreadable. If it seems too wet, add a bit more flour.
3. **Fry the Pancakes:**
   - Heat 2 tablespoons of vegetable oil in a large skillet over medium-high heat.
   - Drop spoonfuls of the batter into the hot oil, flattening them slightly with the back of the spoon to form pancakes.
   - Fry the pancakes for about 3-4 minutes on each side, or until they are golden brown and crispy. Adjust the heat as needed to avoid burning.
4. **Drain and Serve:**
   - Transfer the cooked pancakes to a paper towel-lined plate to drain excess oil.
   - Garnish with chopped fresh chives or parsley if desired.
5. **Serve:**
   - Serve the potato pancakes hot with a dollop of sour cream, applesauce, or a sprinkle of fresh herbs.

Tips:

- For added flavor, you can mix in other ingredients like minced garlic, grated cheese, or chopped bacon.

- If you prefer a less oily pancake, you can bake them in the oven at 425°F (220°C) for about 20-25 minutes, flipping halfway through, until crispy and golden.

Enjoy your **Ziemniaczane Racuchy**! These potato pancakes are crispy on the outside, tender on the inside, and perfect for a comforting meal or snack.

Kluski na Parze (Steamed Dumplings)

Ingredients:

- 500g (about 4 cups) all-purpose flour
- 1 packet (about 7g or 2 1/4 teaspoons) dry yeast
- 1 cup (240ml) warm milk (about 110°F or 45°C)
- 2 tablespoons granulated sugar
- 1/4 cup (60g) unsalted butter, melted
- 1 large egg
- 1 teaspoon salt

Instructions:

1. **Activate the Yeast:**
   - In a small bowl, combine the warm milk and sugar. Stir until the sugar is dissolved.
   - Sprinkle the dry yeast over the milk mixture. Let it sit for about 5-10 minutes, or until the yeast becomes frothy and bubbles.
2. **Prepare the Dough:**
   - In a large mixing bowl, combine the flour and salt.
   - Make a well in the center and pour in the yeast mixture, melted butter, and egg.
   - Mix until a dough forms. Knead the dough on a floured surface for about 5-7 minutes, or until it becomes smooth and elastic. You may need to add a little more flour if the dough is too sticky.
3. **Let the Dough Rise:**
   - Place the dough in a lightly greased bowl and cover it with a clean cloth or plastic wrap.
   - Let the dough rise in a warm, draft-free area for about 1-1.5 hours, or until it has doubled in size.
4. **Shape the Dumplings:**
   - Once the dough has risen, punch it down to release the air.
   - Divide the dough into small portions and shape them into balls or small oval dumplings.
   - Place the dumplings on a lightly floured surface and let them rest for about 15 minutes.
5. **Steam the Dumplings:**
   - Prepare a steamer or a large pot with a steaming rack. Fill the bottom of the pot with a few inches of water and bring it to a boil.
   - Place the dumplings on the steaming rack or a parchment-lined steamer basket, leaving space between them.
   - Cover and steam the dumplings for about 15-20 minutes, or until they are puffed and cooked through.
6. **Serve:**

- Serve the steamed dumplings hot. They pair well with meats, gravies, or as a side dish with vegetables.

Tips:

- If you don't have a steamer, you can use a heatproof plate or dish placed on a rack inside a large pot with a lid.
- For added flavor, you can incorporate herbs or spices into the dough before steaming.

Enjoy your **Kluski na Parze**! These steamed dumplings are soft and airy, making them a versatile addition to any meal.

Sernik na Zimno (No-Bake Cheesecake)

Ingredients:

For the Crust:

- 200g (about 2 cups) digestive biscuits or graham crackers, crushed
- 100g (about 1/2 cup) unsalted butter, melted
- 2 tablespoons granulated sugar (optional)

For the Filling:

- 500g (about 2 cups) cream cheese, softened
- 200g (about 1 cup) powdered sugar
- 1 cup (240ml) heavy cream
- 1 teaspoon vanilla extract
- 1 tablespoon lemon juice
- 1 tablespoon gelatin powder
- 3 tablespoons water (for blooming gelatin)
- 1/4 cup (60ml) boiling water (for dissolving gelatin)

For the Topping (optional):

- Fresh fruit, fruit compote, or fruit syrup
- Fresh mint leaves (for garnish, optional)

Instructions:

1. **Prepare the Crust:**
   - In a medium bowl, combine the crushed digestive biscuits (or graham crackers), melted butter, and sugar (if using).
   - Mix until the crumbs are evenly coated with butter and the mixture resembles wet sand.
   - Press the mixture into the bottom of a springform pan (about 9 inches) to form an even layer. Use the back of a spoon or the bottom of a glass to press it down firmly.
   - Refrigerate the crust while you prepare the filling.
2. **Prepare the Gelatin:**
   - In a small bowl, sprinkle the gelatin powder over 3 tablespoons of water. Let it sit for about 5 minutes to bloom.
   - Dissolve the bloomed gelatin in 1/4 cup of boiling water, stirring until completely dissolved. Let it cool slightly.
3. **Prepare the Filling:**
   - In a large bowl, beat the softened cream cheese and powdered sugar until smooth and creamy.
   - Add the vanilla extract and lemon juice, and mix well.
   - In a separate bowl, whip the heavy cream until stiff peaks form.
   - Gently fold the whipped cream into the cream cheese mixture.

        - Gradually fold in the dissolved gelatin, making sure it's well incorporated.
4. **Assemble the Cheesecake:**
        - Pour the cheesecake filling over the chilled crust in the springform pan. Smooth the top with a spatula.
        - Refrigerate the cheesecake for at least 4 hours, or until it is set. For best results, leave it overnight.
5. **Serve:**
        - Before serving, top with fresh fruit, fruit compote, or fruit syrup if desired.
        - Garnish with fresh mint leaves if you like.

Tips:

- If you prefer a different flavor, you can add a swirl of fruit puree or melted chocolate into the cheesecake filling before setting.
- For an extra creamy texture, use full-fat cream cheese and heavy cream.
- If you don't have a springform pan, you can use a regular round cake pan lined with parchment paper.

Enjoy your **Sernik na Zimno**! This no-bake cheesecake is a delightful and easy dessert that's perfect for any occasion.

Rurki z Kremem (Pastry Tubes with Cream)

Ingredients:

For the Pastry Tubes:

- 1 sheet puff pastry (about 10x10 inches, thawed if frozen)
- 1 egg (for egg wash)
- Powdered sugar (for dusting)

For the Cream Filling:

- 1 cup (240ml) whole milk
- 1/2 cup (100g) granulated sugar
- 1/4 cup (25g) cornstarch
- 1/4 teaspoon salt
- 3 large egg yolks
- 2 tablespoons unsalted butter
- 1 teaspoon vanilla extract

Instructions:

1. **Prepare the Pastry Tubes:**
    - Preheat your oven to 375°F (190°C). Line a baking sheet with parchment paper.
    - Roll out the puff pastry sheet on a lightly floured surface. Cut it into strips about 1 inch wide and 6 inches long.
    - If you have metal or wooden cannoli tubes, you can use them to shape the pastry. Wrap each strip of puff pastry around a cannoli tube, overlapping slightly.
    - Place the wrapped tubes on the prepared baking sheet. Brush the pastry with a beaten egg for a golden finish.
    - Bake in the preheated oven for 15-20 minutes, or until the pastry is golden brown and crispy.
    - Remove the pastry tubes from the oven and let them cool completely. Carefully remove the tubes from the pastries once they are cool.
2. **Prepare the Cream Filling:**
    - In a medium saucepan, combine the milk, sugar, cornstarch, and salt. Whisk until smooth.
    - Heat the mixture over medium heat, whisking constantly until it comes to a boil and thickens.
    - In a separate bowl, whisk the egg yolks.
    - Gradually add a few spoonfuls of the hot milk mixture to the egg yolks, whisking constantly to temper the eggs.
    - Pour the tempered egg yolks back into the saucepan and continue cooking for 2-3 minutes, until the mixture is thick and smooth.

- Remove from heat and stir in the butter and vanilla extract.
- Transfer the cream to a bowl, cover with plastic wrap directly on the surface of the cream to prevent a skin from forming, and let it cool to room temperature.
3. **Fill the Pastry Tubes:**
   - Once the cream filling is cooled, use a piping bag fitted with a small round tip to fill the pastry tubes with the cream.
   - Alternatively, you can use a small spoon or a knife to fill the tubes.
4. **Serve:**
   - Dust the filled pastry tubes with powdered sugar before serving.
   - Enjoy the pastries fresh, as they are best served the same day they are filled.

Tips:

- If you don't have cannoli tubes, you can create your own by wrapping aluminum foil into tube shapes.
- For a variation, you can flavor the cream with a bit of citrus zest or liqueur.

Enjoy your **Rurki z Kremem**! These elegant pastries are perfect for a special treat or as a delightful dessert for any occasion.

Deser Słodki z Kaszy (Sweet Buckwheat Dessert)

Ingredients:

- 1 cup (200g) buckwheat groats
- 2 cups (480ml) milk (or a non-dairy alternative)
- 1/4 cup (50g) granulated sugar (adjust to taste)
- 1/2 teaspoon vanilla extract
- 1/4 teaspoon ground cinnamon
- 1/4 cup (30g) raisins or dried fruits (optional)
- 1/4 cup (30g) chopped nuts (such as walnuts or almonds, optional)
- Fresh or dried fruit for topping (e.g., berries, apples, pears)
- Honey or maple syrup (for drizzling, optional)

Instructions:

1. **Prepare the Buckwheat:**
   - Rinse the buckwheat groats under cold water to remove any impurities.
   - In a medium saucepan, bring 2 cups of water to a boil. Add the rinsed buckwheat and reduce the heat to low.
   - Cover and simmer for about 10-15 minutes, or until the buckwheat is tender and the water is absorbed. If needed, add a bit more water during cooking.
2. **Cook with Milk:**
   - Once the buckwheat is cooked, stir in the milk, sugar, vanilla extract, and ground cinnamon.
   - Cook over medium heat, stirring frequently, until the mixture thickens to a creamy consistency. This should take about 5-10 minutes.
   - If using raisins or dried fruits, stir them in during the last few minutes of cooking so they can plump up.
3. **Add Nuts:**
   - If desired, stir in the chopped nuts just before serving for added texture and flavor.
4. **Serve:**
   - Serve the sweet buckwheat dessert warm or chilled. Top with fresh or dried fruit and a drizzle of honey or maple syrup if desired.

Tips:

- For added flavor, you can mix in a spoonful of fruit preserves or a sprinkle of additional spices like nutmeg.
- You can also experiment with different types of milk or milk alternatives to suit your taste and dietary preferences.
- This dessert is quite versatile and can be adapted to include various fruits and nuts based on what you have on hand.

Enjoy your **Deser Słodki z Kaszy**! This sweet buckwheat dessert offers a delightful, nutty flavor and a comforting, creamy texture, making it a unique and satisfying treat.

Racuchy (Apple Pancakes)

Ingredients:

- 2 medium apples (such as Granny Smith or Honeycrisp)
- 1 cup (120g) all-purpose flour
- 1 tablespoon granulated sugar
- 1/2 teaspoon baking powder
- 1/4 teaspoon baking soda
- 1/4 teaspoon salt
- 1 large egg
- 3/4 cup (180ml) milk
- 1 teaspoon vanilla extract
- 1/2 teaspoon ground cinnamon (optional)
- 2 tablespoons unsalted butter (for frying)
- Powdered sugar (for dusting, optional)
- Sour cream (for serving, optional)

Instructions:

1. **Prepare the Apples:**
   - Peel, core, and dice the apples into small pieces. You can also grate them if you prefer finer apple pieces.
2. **Mix the Batter:**
   - In a large bowl, whisk together the flour, sugar, baking powder, baking soda, salt, and ground cinnamon (if using).
   - In another bowl, beat the egg, then add the milk and vanilla extract.
   - Pour the wet ingredients into the dry ingredients and stir until just combined. The batter should be thick but pourable.
   - Gently fold the diced or grated apples into the batter.
3. **Cook the Pancakes:**
   - Heat a large skillet or griddle over medium heat and add a little butter.
   - Once the butter is melted and bubbly, spoon dollops of batter onto the skillet, spreading them slightly to form pancakes.
   - Cook for about 2-3 minutes on each side, or until the pancakes are golden brown and cooked through.
   - Remove the pancakes from the skillet and keep warm while you cook the remaining batter, adding more butter to the skillet as needed.
4. **Serve:**
   - Dust the apple pancakes with powdered sugar if desired.
   - Serve warm with a dollop of sour cream or your favorite toppings, such as fresh fruit or maple syrup.

Tips:

- For extra flavor, you can mix in a bit of nutmeg or ginger along with the cinnamon.
- If the batter seems too thick, add a splash more milk until it reaches the desired consistency.
- These pancakes can also be enjoyed with a drizzle of honey or a sprinkle of chopped nuts for added texture.

Enjoy your **Racuchy**! These apple pancakes are wonderfully light and fluffy, with a delicious burst of apple flavor in every bite.

Słodki Kołacz (Sweet Kołacz)

Ingredients:

For the Dough:

- 3 1/2 cups (450g) all-purpose flour
- 1/2 cup (100g) granulated sugar
- 1/4 cup (60ml) warm milk (about 110°F or 45°C)
- 1/4 cup (60g) unsalted butter, softened
- 1/4 cup (60ml) sour cream or plain yogurt
- 2 large eggs
- 1 packet (7g or 2 1/4 teaspoons) active dry yeast
- 1/2 teaspoon salt
- 1 teaspoon vanilla extract

For the Filling (optional):

- 1 cup (240ml) fruit preserves (such as apricot, raspberry, or strawberry)
- 1/2 cup (100g) sweetened cream cheese or ricotta cheese (optional)
- 1/4 cup (50g) granulated sugar (optional, if you want a sweetened cream cheese filling)

For the Topping:

- 1 egg (for egg wash)
- 2 tablespoons granulated sugar (optional, for sprinkling)
- Powdered sugar (for dusting, optional)

Instructions:

1. **Prepare the Dough:**
   - In a small bowl, dissolve the yeast in the warm milk with a pinch of sugar. Let it sit for about 5-10 minutes until it becomes frothy.
   - In a large bowl, whisk together the flour, sugar, and salt.
   - Make a well in the center and add the yeast mixture, softened butter, sour cream (or yogurt), eggs, and vanilla extract.
   - Mix until a dough forms, then knead on a floured surface for about 5-7 minutes, until the dough is smooth and elastic.
   - Place the dough in a lightly greased bowl, cover with a cloth or plastic wrap, and let it rise in a warm place for about 1-1.5 hours, or until it has doubled in size.
2. **Shape the Kołacz:**
   - Punch down the dough to release the air. Turn it out onto a lightly floured surface.
   - Roll the dough out into a large rectangle (about 12x18 inches).

- If using a filling, spread it evenly over the dough. If using fruit preserves, you can swirl it into the dough or spread it in a thin layer. If using sweetened cream cheese, spread it over the dough and add the fruit preserves on top.
- Roll the dough up from the long side to form a log. Shape the log into a ring and pinch the ends together to seal.
- Place the ring on a parchment-lined baking sheet.

3. **Proof and Bake:**
   - Cover the ring with a cloth and let it rise for about 30-45 minutes, or until it has puffed up.
   - Preheat your oven to 350°F (175°C).
   - Brush the top of the dough with the beaten egg for a glossy finish. Sprinkle with granulated sugar if desired.
   - Bake for about 25-30 minutes, or until the kołacz is golden brown and sounds hollow when tapped.

4. **Cool and Serve:**
   - Let the kołacz cool on a wire rack.
   - Once cooled, dust with powdered sugar if desired before serving.

Tips:

- You can also add spices like cinnamon or cardamom to the dough for extra flavor.
- Feel free to experiment with different fillings, such as chocolate, nuts, or poppy seeds.

Enjoy your **Słodki Kołacz**! This sweet, yeasted bread is perfect for any special occasion or as a delightful treat to enjoy with family and friends.

Ciasto Drożdżowe z Owocami (Yeast Cake with Fruit)

Ingredients:

For the Dough:

- 3 1/2 cups (450g) all-purpose flour
- 1/2 cup (100g) granulated sugar
- 1/2 cup (120ml) warm milk (about 110°F or 45°C)
- 1/4 cup (60g) unsalted butter, softened
- 2 large eggs
- 1 packet (7g or 2 1/4 teaspoons) active dry yeast
- 1/4 teaspoon salt
- 1 teaspoon vanilla extract

For the Fruit Topping:

- 2 cups (about 300g) fresh fruit (such as berries, diced apples, or sliced stone fruits) or 1 cup (about 200g) fruit preserves
- 2 tablespoons granulated sugar (for sprinkling on top of the fruit)

For the Streusel Topping (optional):

- 1/2 cup (60g) all-purpose flour
- 1/4 cup (50g) granulated sugar
- 1/4 cup (60g) unsalted butter, cold and cut into small pieces

For the Glaze (optional):

- 1/2 cup (60g) powdered sugar
- 1-2 tablespoons milk or lemon juice

Instructions:

1. **Prepare the Dough:**
    - In a small bowl, dissolve the yeast in the warm milk with a pinch of sugar. Let it sit for about 5-10 minutes until it becomes frothy.
    - In a large bowl, whisk together the flour, sugar, and salt.
    - Make a well in the center and add the yeast mixture, softened butter, eggs, and vanilla extract.
    - Mix until a dough forms. Knead on a floured surface for about 5-7 minutes, until the dough is smooth and elastic.
    - Place the dough in a lightly greased bowl, cover with a cloth or plastic wrap, and let it rise in a warm place for about 1-1.5 hours, or until it has doubled in size.
2. **Prepare the Fruit and Streusel Topping:**
    - If using fresh fruit, wash, peel, and slice it as needed. Toss the fruit with a bit of sugar if desired.

- For the streusel topping, in a small bowl, combine the flour, sugar, and cold butter. Use a pastry cutter or your fingers to mix until the mixture resembles coarse crumbs. Set aside.

3. **Shape and Assemble:**
   - Punch down the dough to release the air and turn it out onto a floured surface.
   - Roll the dough out into a rectangle or shape it to fit into a greased or parchment-lined baking pan (about 9x13 inches).
   - Transfer the dough to the prepared pan and spread it out evenly.
   - Top the dough with the fresh fruit or fruit preserves. If using preserves, spread it in an even layer over the dough.
   - Sprinkle the streusel topping over the fruit if using.

4. **Proof and Bake:**
   - Cover the pan with a cloth and let the dough rise for about 30-45 minutes, or until it has puffed up.
   - Preheat your oven to 350°F (175°C).
   - Bake for about 30-40 minutes, or until the cake is golden brown and a toothpick inserted into the center comes out clean.

5. **Cool and Glaze (Optional):**
   - Let the cake cool in the pan for about 10 minutes, then transfer it to a wire rack to cool completely.
   - If desired, mix the powdered sugar with 1-2 tablespoons of milk or lemon juice to create a glaze. Drizzle the glaze over the cooled cake.

Tips:

- You can experiment with different types of fruit depending on the season and your preference.
- For a richer flavor, you can add a pinch of ground cinnamon to the dough or streusel topping.

Enjoy your **Ciasto Drożdżowe z Owocami**! This yeast cake with fruit is a delicious, versatile dessert that combines a soft, fluffy cake with the sweetness and tartness of fresh or preserved fruit.

Babeczki (Cupcakes)

Ingredients:

For the Cupcakes:

- 1 1/2 cups (190g) all-purpose flour
- 1 cup (200g) granulated sugar
- 1/2 cup (115g) unsalted butter, softened
- 2 large eggs
- 1/2 cup (120ml) milk
- 1 1/2 teaspoons baking powder
- 1/4 teaspoon salt
- 1 teaspoon vanilla extract

For the Frosting:

- 1/2 cup (115g) unsalted butter, softened
- 2 cups (240g) powdered sugar
- 2 tablespoons milk (more if needed)
- 1 teaspoon vanilla extract
- Food coloring (optional)

Instructions:

1. **Prepare the Cupcake Batter:**
    - Preheat your oven to 350°F (175°C). Line a muffin tin with paper cupcake liners.
    - In a medium bowl, whisk together the flour, baking powder, and salt.
    - In a large bowl, cream the softened butter and granulated sugar until light and fluffy.
    - Add the eggs one at a time, beating well after each addition. Mix in the vanilla extract.
    - Gradually add the flour mixture to the butter mixture, alternating with the milk. Start and end with the flour mixture, mixing until just combined.
    - Spoon the batter into the prepared cupcake liners, filling each about 2/3 full.
2. **Bake the Cupcakes:**
    - Bake in the preheated oven for 18-20 minutes, or until a toothpick inserted into the center of a cupcake comes out clean.
    - Allow the cupcakes to cool in the tin for 5 minutes, then transfer them to a wire rack to cool completely before frosting.
3. **Prepare the Frosting:**
    - In a medium bowl, beat the softened butter until creamy.
    - Gradually add the powdered sugar, mixing well after each addition.

- Add the milk and vanilla extract, and continue to beat until the frosting is smooth and spreadable. Add more milk if needed to reach the desired consistency.
- If using food coloring, divide the frosting into bowls and mix in the coloring to your liking.

4. **Frost the Cupcakes:**
   - Once the cupcakes are completely cooled, frost them with the prepared frosting. You can use a knife, spatula, or piping bag with a decorative tip for a more polished look.
   - Optional: Decorate with sprinkles, edible glitter, or other toppings of your choice.

Tips:

- For an extra flavor twist, you can add lemon zest, almond extract, or other flavorings to the batter.
- To make these cupcakes even more special, try adding fruit preserves or chocolate chips to the batter before baking.

Enjoy your **Babeczki**! These cupcakes are soft, fluffy, and perfect for any celebration or as a sweet treat any time of the day.

Tarta z Owocami (Fruit Tart)

Ingredients:

For the Tart Crust:

- 1 1/2 cups (190g) all-purpose flour
- 1/2 cup (100g) granulated sugar
- 1/2 cup (115g) unsalted butter, cold and cut into small pieces
- 1 large egg yolk
- 1-2 tablespoons ice water (as needed)

For the Pastry Cream Filling:

- 2 cups (480ml) whole milk
- 1/2 cup (100g) granulated sugar
- 1/4 cup (25g) cornstarch
- 1/4 teaspoon salt
- 4 large egg yolks
- 2 tablespoons unsalted butter
- 1 teaspoon vanilla extract

For the Topping:

- 2 cups (about 300g) fresh fruit (such as strawberries, blueberries, kiwi, raspberries, or any seasonal fruit)
- 1/4 cup (60ml) apricot glaze or fruit preserves (optional, for a shiny finish)

Instructions:

1. **Prepare the Tart Crust:**
    - In a food processor, combine the flour and sugar. Add the cold butter and pulse until the mixture resembles coarse crumbs.
    - Add the egg yolk and pulse a few more times until the mixture starts to come together. If needed, add 1-2 tablespoons of ice water, a little at a time, until the dough just begins to form.
    - Turn the dough out onto a lightly floured surface and knead it a few times until smooth. Flatten it into a disk, wrap it in plastic wrap, and refrigerate for at least 30 minutes.
2. **Preheat the Oven and Bake the Crust:**
    - Preheat your oven to 375°F (190°C).
    - Roll out the chilled dough on a lightly floured surface to fit a 9-inch tart pan. Carefully transfer the dough to the tart pan, pressing it into the bottom and sides. Trim any excess dough.
    - Line the dough with parchment paper and fill with pie weights or dried beans.
    - Bake in the preheated oven for 15 minutes. Remove the parchment and weights, then bake for an additional 5-7 minutes, or until the crust is golden brown. Let it cool completely.

3. **Prepare the Pastry Cream Filling:**
    - In a medium saucepan, heat the milk over medium heat until it is just about to boil.
    - In a separate bowl, whisk together the sugar, cornstarch, and salt. Whisk in the egg yolks until smooth.
    - Gradually add the hot milk to the egg mixture, whisking constantly to temper the eggs.
    - Return the mixture to the saucepan and cook over medium heat, whisking constantly, until it thickens and comes to a boil.
    - Remove from heat and stir in the butter and vanilla extract. Continue to stir until the butter is fully melted and incorporated.
    - Transfer the pastry cream to a bowl, cover with plastic wrap directly on the surface of the cream to prevent a skin from forming, and let it cool to room temperature.
4. **Assemble the Tart:**
    - Spread the cooled pastry cream evenly over the baked tart crust.
    - Arrange the fresh fruit on top of the pastry cream in a decorative pattern.
    - If desired, heat the apricot glaze or fruit preserves until liquid, then brush it over the fruit to give it a shiny finish.
5. **Serve:**
    - Chill the tart in the refrigerator for at least 1 hour before serving to allow the pastry cream to set and the flavors to meld.

Tips:

- You can use any combination of fresh fruit based on what is in season or your personal preference.
- For a more intense fruit flavor, consider adding a layer of fruit preserves under the pastry cream before adding the fresh fruit.

Enjoy your **Tarta z Owocami**! This fruit tart is a stunning and delicious dessert that combines a buttery crust, creamy filling, and vibrant fresh fruit, making it perfect for any occasion.

Keks (Fruit Cake)

Ingredients:

For the Cake:

- 1 cup (150g) mixed dried fruit (such as raisins, currants, chopped dried apricots, or dates)
- 1/2 cup (75g) chopped nuts (such as walnuts, almonds, or pecans)
- 1/2 cup (120ml) orange juice
- 1/2 cup (115g) unsalted butter, softened
- 1 cup (200g) granulated sugar
- 4 large eggs
- 1 1/2 cups (190g) all-purpose flour
- 1 teaspoon baking powder
- 1/2 teaspoon ground cinnamon
- 1/4 teaspoon ground cloves
- 1/4 teaspoon salt
- 1/4 cup (60ml) brandy or rum (optional, for soaking fruit)

For the Glaze (optional):

- 1/4 cup (60ml) apricot glaze or fruit preserves
- 1 tablespoon water

Instructions:

1. **Prepare the Fruit and Nuts:**
     - If using brandy or rum, soak the dried fruit in the alcohol for at least 1 hour or overnight. Drain the fruit before using.
     - Preheat your oven to 325°F (165°C). Grease and line a 9-inch (23cm) loaf pan with parchment paper.
2. **Mix the Cake Batter:**
     - In a medium bowl, whisk together the flour, baking powder, cinnamon, cloves, and salt.
     - In a large bowl, cream the softened butter and sugar until light and fluffy.
     - Add the eggs one at a time, beating well after each addition.
     - Gradually add the flour mixture to the butter mixture, mixing until just combined.
     - Stir in the orange juice, soaked dried fruit (and nuts, if using), until evenly distributed.
3. **Bake the Cake:**
     - Pour the batter into the prepared loaf pan and smooth the top.
     - Bake in the preheated oven for about 60-70 minutes, or until a toothpick inserted into the center comes out clean.

- Allow the cake to cool in the pan for about 10 minutes, then transfer it to a wire rack to cool completely.
4. **Prepare the Glaze (optional):**
    - If using a glaze, heat the apricot preserves and water in a small saucepan over low heat until smooth and thin.
    - Brush the glaze over the cooled cake to give it a shiny finish.
5. **Serve:**
    - Slice the fruit cake and serve. It's delicious on its own or with a cup of tea or coffee.

Tips:

- Feel free to experiment with different combinations of dried fruits and nuts based on your preference.
- The fruit cake can be made ahead of time and stored in an airtight container. It often tastes even better after a few days as the flavors meld.

Enjoy your **Keks**! This fruit cake is a wonderful blend of sweet and spicy flavors with a moist texture, making it a delightful treat for any occasion.

Ciasto Puchowe (Fluffy Cake)

Ingredients:

For the Cake:

- 1 cup (200g) granulated sugar
- 1 cup (120g) all-purpose flour
- 4 large eggs, separated
- 1/2 cup (120ml) milk
- 1/2 cup (115g) unsalted butter, melted and slightly cooled
- 1 tablespoon baking powder
- 1/4 teaspoon salt
- 1 teaspoon vanilla extract
- 1/2 teaspoon cream of tartar (optional, helps stabilize the egg whites)

For Dusting:

- Powdered sugar (optional)

For Topping (optional):

- Fresh fruit, fruit preserves, or a simple glaze

Instructions:

1. **Preheat the Oven:**
    - Preheat your oven to 350°F (175°C). Grease and flour an 8-inch (20cm) round cake pan or line it with parchment paper.
2. **Prepare the Batter:**
    - In a medium bowl, sift together the flour, baking powder, and salt.
    - In a large bowl, beat the egg yolks and granulated sugar until light and fluffy. Add the vanilla extract.
    - Gradually add the melted butter and milk to the egg yolk mixture, mixing until combined.
    - Gently fold in the dry ingredients until just combined.
3. **Whip the Egg Whites:**
    - In a clean bowl, beat the egg whites with an electric mixer on medium speed until frothy. If using, add the cream of tartar.
    - Increase the mixer speed and beat until stiff peaks form. The egg whites should be glossy and hold their shape.
4. **Combine and Fold:**
    - Gently fold the whipped egg whites into the cake batter in thirds, being careful not to deflate the mixture. Use a spatula and fold gently until the batter is smooth and combined.

5. **Bake the Cake:**
    - Pour the batter into the prepared cake pan and smooth the top.
    - Bake in the preheated oven for 25-30 minutes, or until the cake is golden brown and a toothpick inserted into the center comes out clean.
    - Allow the cake to cool in the pan for about 10 minutes, then transfer it to a wire rack to cool completely.
6. **Serve:**
    - Once the cake is completely cool, dust with powdered sugar if desired.
    - You can also top the cake with fresh fruit, fruit preserves, or a simple glaze if you like.

Tips:

- For an extra light and airy cake, ensure that your mixing bowls and beaters are clean and free from any grease or oil when whipping the egg whites.
- If you prefer a flavored cake, you can add a bit of lemon zest or almond extract to the batter.

Enjoy your **Ciasto Puchowe**! This fluffy cake is wonderfully light and versatile, making it a delightful treat for any occasion.

Kisiel (Fruit Jelly)

Ingredients:

For the Fruit Base:

- 2 cups (480ml) fruit juice (such as apple, grape, raspberry, or cranberry) or fruit puree
- 1/2 cup (100g) granulated sugar (adjust according to the sweetness of the fruit juice or puree)
- 1 tablespoon lemon juice (optional, for a tangy flavor)

For Thickening:

- 3 tablespoons cornstarch
- 1/4 cup (60ml) cold water

For Garnish (optional):

- Fresh fruit pieces or berries
- Mint leaves

Instructions:

1. **Prepare the Fruit Base:**
    - In a medium saucepan, combine the fruit juice or puree with the granulated sugar and lemon juice (if using). Heat over medium heat, stirring occasionally, until the sugar is completely dissolved and the mixture is warm.
2. **Make the Slurry:**
    - In a small bowl, mix the cornstarch with the cold water to create a smooth slurry. This will be used to thicken the fruit base.
3. **Thicken the Kisiel:**
    - Slowly pour the cornstarch slurry into the warm fruit mixture while stirring continuously to prevent lumps.
    - Continue to cook the mixture over medium heat, stirring constantly, until it thickens and becomes translucent. This should take about 2-3 minutes.
4. **Cool and Set:**
    - Once thickened, remove the saucepan from the heat. Let the Kisiel cool slightly before transferring it to serving dishes or bowls.
    - Refrigerate the Kisiel for at least 2 hours, or until it is fully set and chilled.
5. **Serve:**
    - Serve the Kisiel chilled. You can garnish with fresh fruit pieces or berries, and a sprig of mint if desired.

Tips:

- For a more intense fruit flavor, you can use fruit puree instead of fruit juice.
- Adjust the amount of sugar based on the sweetness of the fruit juice or puree and your personal preference.
- You can also make Kisiel with mixed fruit juices or add a bit of fruit zest for extra flavor.

Enjoy your **Kisiel**! This fruit jelly is a refreshing and versatile dessert that is easy to make and perfect for any season.

Tiramisu (Polish Style)

Ingredients:

For the Cream Mixture:

- 1 cup (240ml) heavy cream
- 1 cup (250g) mascarpone cheese
- 1/2 cup (100g) granulated sugar
- 2 large egg yolks
- 1 teaspoon vanilla extract

For the Coffee Mixture:

- 1 cup (240ml) strong brewed coffee, cooled to room temperature
- 2 tablespoons coffee liqueur or dark rum (optional, for extra flavor)

For Assembly:

- 24-30 ladyfingers (savoiardi)
- Cocoa powder, for dusting
- Chocolate shavings or grated chocolate (optional, for garnish)

Instructions:

1. **Prepare the Coffee Mixture:**
   - In a shallow dish, combine the cooled coffee with the coffee liqueur or dark rum (if using). Set aside.
2. **Make the Cream Mixture:**
   - In a medium bowl, beat the heavy cream until soft peaks form. Set aside.
   - In another bowl, whisk the egg yolks and granulated sugar together until pale and creamy.
   - Add the mascarpone cheese and vanilla extract to the egg yolk mixture and mix until smooth.
   - Gently fold the whipped cream into the mascarpone mixture until fully combined and smooth.
3. **Assemble the Tiramisu:**
   - Quickly dip each ladyfinger into the coffee mixture, ensuring they are soaked but not overly soggy.
   - Arrange a layer of soaked ladyfingers in the bottom of your serving dish (a 9x9-inch or similar size works well).
   - Spread half of the mascarpone cream mixture evenly over the ladyfingers.
   - Add another layer of soaked ladyfingers on top of the cream.
   - Spread the remaining mascarpone cream mixture evenly over the second layer of ladyfingers.

4. **Chill and Serve:**
    - Cover the tiramisu with plastic wrap and refrigerate for at least 4 hours, or overnight if possible, to allow the flavors to meld and the dessert to set.
    - Before serving, dust the top with cocoa powder and garnish with chocolate shavings or grated chocolate if desired.

Tips:

- For a less intense coffee flavor, you can reduce the amount of coffee or omit the coffee liqueur.
- Ensure the coffee is cooled to room temperature before dipping the ladyfingers to prevent them from becoming too mushy.
- If you prefer a non-alcoholic version, simply omit the coffee liqueur or rum.

Enjoy your **Tiramisu** Polish-style! This dessert is a luxurious treat with its creamy, coffee-infused layers, perfect for any occasion.

Orzechowiec (Nut Cake)

Ingredients:

For the Cake:

- 1 1/2 cups (150g) ground walnuts or hazelnuts (or a mix)
- 1 cup (200g) granulated sugar
- 1 cup (120g) all-purpose flour
- 4 large eggs, separated
- 1/2 cup (115g) unsalted butter, melted
- 1 teaspoon vanilla extract
- 1 teaspoon baking powder
- 1/4 teaspoon salt

For the Cream Filling (optional):

- 1 cup (240ml) heavy cream
- 2 tablespoons powdered sugar
- 1 teaspoon vanilla extract

For Garnish (optional):

- Chopped nuts
- Powdered sugar

Instructions:

1. **Preheat the Oven:**
    - Preheat your oven to 350°F (175°C). Grease and flour a 9-inch (23cm) round cake pan or line it with parchment paper.
2. **Prepare the Cake Batter:**
    - In a medium bowl, whisk together the flour, baking powder, and salt. Set aside.
    - In a large bowl, beat the egg yolks and granulated sugar until light and fluffy.
    - Stir in the melted butter and vanilla extract.
    - Gradually add the ground nuts to the egg yolk mixture, mixing until well combined.
    - In a separate bowl, beat the egg whites until stiff peaks form. Gently fold the egg whites into the nut mixture in thirds, being careful not to deflate the mixture.
3. **Bake the Cake:**
    - Pour the batter into the prepared cake pan and smooth the top.
    - Bake in the preheated oven for about 30-35 minutes, or until the cake is golden brown and a toothpick inserted into the center comes out clean.
    - Allow the cake to cool in the pan for 10 minutes, then transfer it to a wire rack to cool completely.

4. **Prepare the Cream Filling (if using):**
    - In a medium bowl, beat the heavy cream with powdered sugar and vanilla extract until stiff peaks form.
    - Spread the whipped cream evenly over the top of the cooled cake or between layers if you are making a layered cake.
5. **Garnish and Serve:**
    - Garnish the cake with chopped nuts and a dusting of powdered sugar if desired.
    - Slice and serve. The cake can be enjoyed as is or with a cup of tea or coffee.

Tips:

- For a richer flavor, you can toast the ground nuts lightly before adding them to the batter.
- If you prefer, you can use a combination of nuts, such as walnuts and hazelnuts, for a more complex flavor.
- The nut cake can be served plain or with the cream filling and garnish, depending on your preference.

Enjoy your **Orzechowiec**! This nut cake is a delightful and flavorful dessert that's sure to please anyone who loves rich, nutty flavors.

Czekoladowe Muffinki (Chocolate Muffins)

Ingredients:

For the Muffins:

- 1 3/4 cups (220g) all-purpose flour
- 1/2 cup (50g) unsweetened cocoa powder
- 1 cup (200g) granulated sugar
- 2 teaspoons baking powder
- 1/2 teaspoon baking soda
- 1/4 teaspoon salt
- 1/2 cup (115g) unsalted butter, melted
- 2 large eggs
- 1 cup (240ml) milk
- 1 teaspoon vanilla extract
- 1/2 cup (90g) chocolate chips or chopped chocolate (optional, for extra chocolatey goodness)

For the Topping (optional):

- Additional chocolate chips or chopped chocolate
- Sugar for sprinkling

Instructions:

1. **Preheat the Oven:**
    - Preheat your oven to 350°F (175°C). Line a muffin tin with paper liners or lightly grease it.
2. **Prepare the Dry Ingredients:**
    - In a large bowl, whisk together the flour, cocoa powder, sugar, baking powder, baking soda, and salt.
3. **Prepare the Wet Ingredients:**
    - In another bowl, whisk together the melted butter, eggs, milk, and vanilla extract until well combined.
4. **Combine the Mixtures:**
    - Pour the wet ingredients into the dry ingredients and gently fold until just combined. Be careful not to overmix; the batter should be lumpy.
    - Fold in the chocolate chips or chopped chocolate, if using.
5. **Fill the Muffin Tin:**
    - Divide the batter evenly among the muffin cups, filling each about 2/3 full. If desired, sprinkle a few additional chocolate chips on top of each muffin.
6. **Bake the Muffins:**

- Bake in the preheated oven for 18-22 minutes, or until a toothpick inserted into the center comes out clean or with a few moist crumbs.
- Allow the muffins to cool in the pan for 5 minutes, then transfer them to a wire rack to cool completely.

7. **Serve:**
   - Enjoy the muffins warm or at room temperature. They are perfect on their own or with a glass of milk or a cup of coffee.

Tips:

- For an extra touch, you can add a swirl of peanut butter or Nutella to the batter before baking.
- To ensure the muffins are extra moist, be careful not to overmix the batter. It's okay if there are a few lumps.
- Store any leftover muffins in an airtight container at room temperature for up to 3 days or freeze for longer storage.

Enjoy your **Czekoladowe Muffinki**! These chocolate muffins are rich, chocolatey, and wonderfully fluffy, making them a delightful treat for any occasion.

Kokosanki (Coconut Macaroons)

Ingredients:

- 2 1/2 cups (200g) shredded coconut (sweetened or unsweetened, based on preference)
- 1 cup (240ml) sweetened condensed milk
- 1/2 teaspoon vanilla extract
- 1/4 teaspoon almond extract (optional, for added flavor)
- A pinch of salt
- 2 large egg whites
- 1/4 cup (50g) granulated sugar

For Dipping (optional):

- 1/2 cup (90g) semi-sweet or dark chocolate chips
- 1 teaspoon coconut oil or vegetable oil (optional, to thin the chocolate for dipping)

Instructions:

1. **Preheat the Oven:**
   - Preheat your oven to 350°F (175°C). Line a baking sheet with parchment paper or a silicone baking mat.
2. **Prepare the Coconut Mixture:**
   - In a large bowl, combine the shredded coconut, sweetened condensed milk, vanilla extract, almond extract (if using), and a pinch of salt. Mix until well combined.
3. **Whip the Egg Whites:**
   - In a separate clean bowl, beat the egg whites with an electric mixer until frothy. Gradually add the granulated sugar and continue to beat until stiff peaks form.
4. **Fold the Mixtures Together:**
   - Gently fold the whipped egg whites into the coconut mixture. Be careful not to overmix; fold until the mixture is just combined.
5. **Shape the Macaroons:**
   - Using a spoon or a small cookie scoop, drop rounded mounds of the mixture onto the prepared baking sheet, spacing them about 1 inch apart.
6. **Bake the Macaroons:**
   - Bake in the preheated oven for 15-20 minutes, or until the macaroons are golden brown on the edges and slightly golden on top.
   - Allow the macaroons to cool on the baking sheet for a few minutes before transferring them to a wire rack to cool completely.
7. **Optional Chocolate Dipping:**
   - If desired, melt the chocolate chips with the coconut oil in a microwave-safe bowl in 20-second intervals, stirring after each interval until smooth.

- Dip the cooled macaroons halfway into the melted chocolate and place them back on the parchment-lined baking sheet. Let the chocolate set before serving.

Tips:

- For added texture and flavor, you can mix in some chopped nuts or dried fruit into the coconut mixture.
- Ensure the mixing bowls and beaters are clean and free from any grease when whipping the egg whites to achieve the best volume.

Enjoy your **Kokosanki**! These coconut macaroons are wonderfully chewy with a sweet coconut flavor and can be enjoyed on their own or with a chocolate dip for an extra touch of indulgence.

Ciasto Kakaowe (Cocoa Cake)

Ingredients:

For the Cake:

- 1 1/2 cups (190g) all-purpose flour
- 1 cup (200g) granulated sugar
- 1/2 cup (50g) unsweetened cocoa powder
- 1 1/2 teaspoons baking powder
- 1/2 teaspoon baking soda
- 1/4 teaspoon salt
- 1/2 cup (120ml) vegetable oil
- 1 cup (240ml) buttermilk or milk
- 2 large eggs
- 1 teaspoon vanilla extract
- 1 cup (240ml) boiling water

For the Frosting (optional):

- 1/2 cup (115g) unsalted butter, softened
- 1/4 cup (50g) unsweetened cocoa powder
- 2 cups (250g) powdered sugar
- 2 tablespoons milk
- 1 teaspoon vanilla extract

Instructions:

1. **Preheat the Oven:**
   - Preheat your oven to 350°F (175°C). Grease and flour an 8-inch (20cm) round cake pan or line it with parchment paper.
2. **Prepare the Dry Ingredients:**
   - In a large bowl, whisk together the flour, sugar, cocoa powder, baking powder, baking soda, and salt.
3. **Mix the Wet Ingredients:**
   - In a separate bowl, combine the vegetable oil, buttermilk (or milk), eggs, and vanilla extract. Mix well.
4. **Combine and Mix:**
   - Gradually add the wet ingredients to the dry ingredients, mixing until just combined.
   - Carefully stir in the boiling water. The batter will be quite thin, but this is normal.
5. **Bake the Cake:**
   - Pour the batter into the prepared cake pan and smooth the top.

- Bake in the preheated oven for 30-35 minutes, or until a toothpick inserted into the center comes out clean.
    - Allow the cake to cool in the pan for 10 minutes, then transfer it to a wire rack to cool completely.
6. **Prepare the Frosting (if using):**
    - In a medium bowl, beat the softened butter until creamy.
    - Gradually add the cocoa powder and powdered sugar, mixing well.
    - Add the milk and vanilla extract and continue to beat until the frosting is smooth and spreadable.
7. **Frost the Cake:**
    - Once the cake has cooled completely, spread the frosting evenly over the top and sides of the cake.

Tips:

- For a richer chocolate flavor, you can use dark cocoa powder or add chocolate chips to the batter.
- You can also add a layer of jam or a filling between cake layers if you're making a layered cake.
- If you prefer a dusted cake, simply sprinkle powdered sugar over the top instead of frosting.

Enjoy your **Ciasto Kakaowe**! This cocoa cake is wonderfully moist and chocolatey, making it a delightful treat for any chocolate lover.

Tort Śmietanowy (Cream Cake)

Ingredients:

For the Cake:

- 4 large eggs
- 1 cup (200g) granulated sugar
- 1 cup (120g) all-purpose flour
- 1 teaspoon baking powder
- 1/2 teaspoon vanilla extract

For the Cream Filling:

- 2 cups (480ml) heavy cream
- 1/2 cup (60g) powdered sugar
- 1 teaspoon vanilla extract

For Assembly:

- 1/2 cup (120ml) fruit jam or preserve (such as raspberry, strawberry, or apricot)
- Fresh fruit (such as strawberries, raspberries, or kiwi), for garnish

Optional:

- 1/4 cup (60ml) liqueur or fruit juice (for soaking the cake layers)

Instructions:

1. **Preheat the Oven:**
   - Preheat your oven to 350°F (175°C). Grease and flour two 8-inch (20cm) round cake pans or line them with parchment paper.
2. **Prepare the Cake Batter:**
   - In a large bowl, beat the eggs and granulated sugar until light and fluffy.
   - Add the vanilla extract.
   - In a separate bowl, sift together the flour and baking powder.
   - Gently fold the dry ingredients into the egg mixture until just combined. Be careful not to overmix.
3. **Bake the Cake:**
   - Divide the batter evenly between the prepared cake pans and smooth the tops.
   - Bake in the preheated oven for 20-25 minutes, or until a toothpick inserted into the center comes out clean.
   - Allow the cakes to cool in the pans for 10 minutes, then transfer them to a wire rack to cool completely.
4. **Prepare the Cream Filling:**
   - In a large bowl, beat the heavy cream, powdered sugar, and vanilla extract until stiff peaks form.
5. **Assemble the Cake:**

- If desired, soak the cake layers lightly with liqueur or fruit juice for added moisture.
- Place one layer of cake on a serving platter. Spread a layer of fruit jam or preserve over the cake layer.
- Spread a generous layer of whipped cream over the jam.
- Place the second cake layer on top and spread whipped cream over the top and sides of the cake.

6. **Garnish:**
   - Garnish with fresh fruit and additional jam or preserve if desired.
7. **Chill and Serve:**
   - Refrigerate the cake for at least 1 hour to allow the flavors to meld and the cream to set.
   - Slice and serve chilled.

Tips:

- For a more decorated cake, you can pipe additional whipped cream decorations on top and around the edges.
- Experiment with different fruits or even add a layer of fresh fruit between the cake layers for added texture and flavor.
- If you prefer a denser cake, you can use a sponge cake recipe or a store-bought sponge cake.

Enjoy your **Tort Śmietanowy**! This cream cake is light, airy, and perfectly balanced with sweet cream and fruit, making it a delightful treat for any occasion.

Ciasto Serowo-Malina (Cheese-Raspberry Cake)

Ingredients:

For the Crust:

- 1 1/2 cups (150g) graham cracker crumbs or crushed digestive biscuits
- 1/4 cup (50g) granulated sugar
- 1/2 cup (115g) unsalted butter, melted

For the Filling:

- 16 oz (450g) cream cheese, softened
- 1 cup (200g) granulated sugar
- 1 teaspoon vanilla extract
- 3 large eggs
- 1 cup (240ml) sour cream or Greek yogurt
- 1/2 cup (120ml) heavy cream

For the Raspberry Swirl:

- 1 cup (120g) fresh or frozen raspberries
- 1/4 cup (50g) granulated sugar
- 1 tablespoon lemon juice

Instructions:

1. **Prepare the Crust:**
   - Preheat your oven to 325°F (163°C). Grease a 9-inch (23cm) springform pan or line it with parchment paper.
   - In a medium bowl, combine the graham cracker crumbs, granulated sugar, and melted butter. Mix until the crumbs are well coated.
   - Press the mixture firmly into the bottom of the prepared pan to form an even layer.
   - Bake the crust in the preheated oven for 10 minutes, then remove it from the oven and let it cool slightly.
2. **Prepare the Raspberry Swirl:**
   - In a small saucepan, combine the raspberries, granulated sugar, and lemon juice. Cook over medium heat, stirring occasionally, until the raspberries break down and the mixture thickens, about 5-7 minutes.
   - Let the raspberry sauce cool to room temperature. You can blend it if you prefer a smoother texture.
3. **Prepare the Filling:**
   - In a large bowl, beat the cream cheese until smooth and creamy.
   - Add the granulated sugar and vanilla extract, and beat until well combined.

- Add the eggs one at a time, beating well after each addition.
- Mix in the sour cream (or Greek yogurt) and heavy cream until the mixture is smooth and well combined.

4. **Assemble the Cake:**
   - Pour the cream cheese filling over the cooled crust in the springform pan.
   - Spoon dollops of the raspberry sauce over the cream cheese filling.
   - Use a knife or a skewer to gently swirl the raspberry sauce into the cream cheese filling for a marbled effect.

5. **Bake the Cake:**
   - Bake in the preheated oven for 55-65 minutes, or until the center is set and the edges are lightly golden.
   - Turn off the oven and crack the oven door slightly. Let the cake cool in the oven for 1 hour.
   - Remove the cake from the oven and refrigerate it for at least 4 hours, or preferably overnight, to allow it to set and develop flavor.

6. **Serve:**
   - Remove the sides of the springform pan before serving.
   - Garnish with additional fresh raspberries if desired.

Tips:

- Make sure all ingredients, especially the cream cheese, are at room temperature before starting to ensure a smooth filling.
- To prevent cracks in the cheesecake, avoid overmixing and try to minimize the amount of air incorporated into the batter.
- If using frozen raspberries, make sure they are thawed and drained to avoid excess moisture in the raspberry sauce.

Enjoy your **Ciasto Serowo-Malina**! This cheese-raspberry cake is a delightful combination of creamy and tart flavors, making it a perfect dessert for any occasion.

Mazurek (Easter Cake)

Ingredients:

For the Crust:

- 2 cups (250g) all-purpose flour
- 1/2 cup (100g) granulated sugar
- 1/2 teaspoon baking powder
- 1/4 teaspoon salt
- 1/2 cup (115g) unsalted butter, cold and cut into small pieces
- 1 large egg yolk
- 2-3 tablespoons cold water

For the Filling:

- 1/2 cup (120ml) fruit preserves or jam (apricot, raspberry, or any fruit flavor you prefer)
- 1/2 cup (100g) granulated sugar
- 1/4 cup (60ml) heavy cream
- 1/4 cup (60g) unsalted butter
- 1 cup (100g) chopped nuts (walnuts, almonds, or hazelnuts)

For the Glaze:

- 1/2 cup (60g) powdered sugar
- 1-2 tablespoons milk or lemon juice
- Optional: additional nuts or candied fruit for decoration

Instructions:

1. **Prepare the Crust:**
    - In a large bowl, whisk together the flour, granulated sugar, baking powder, and salt.
    - Cut in the cold butter using a pastry cutter or your fingers until the mixture resembles coarse crumbs.
    - Add the egg yolk and mix until combined.
    - Gradually add cold water, one tablespoon at a time, until the dough comes together.
    - Form the dough into a disk, wrap it in plastic wrap, and refrigerate for at least 30 minutes.
2. **Preheat the Oven:**
    - Preheat your oven to 350°F (175°C). Grease or line a 9-inch (23cm) tart pan or baking dish with parchment paper.
3. **Roll and Pre-bake the Crust:**
    - On a lightly floured surface, roll out the chilled dough to fit the prepared pan.

- Transfer the dough to the pan, pressing it into the bottom and up the sides.
- Prick the bottom of the crust with a fork to prevent bubbling.
- Bake in the preheated oven for 15-20 minutes, or until lightly golden. Remove from the oven and let it cool slightly.

4. **Prepare the Filling:**
    - In a small saucepan, combine the fruit preserves, granulated sugar, heavy cream, and butter. Cook over medium heat, stirring frequently, until the mixture is smooth and slightly thickened.
    - Stir in the chopped nuts.

5. **Assemble and Bake:**
    - Spread the fruit and nut mixture evenly over the pre-baked crust.
    - Return the pan to the oven and bake for an additional 10-15 minutes, or until the filling is bubbly and the nuts are lightly toasted.

6. **Prepare the Glaze:**
    - In a small bowl, whisk together the powdered sugar and milk or lemon juice until smooth.
    - Drizzle the glaze over the cooled Mazurek.

7. **Decorate and Serve:**
    - Optionally, garnish with additional nuts or candied fruit before the glaze sets.
    - Allow the cake to cool completely before slicing and serving.

Tips:

- You can customize the filling by using different types of fruit preserves or adding spices such as cinnamon or cloves.
- For a more decorative touch, you can use cookie cutters to cut shapes from additional dough and place them on top of the filling before baking.
- Ensure the Mazurek is fully cooled before applying the glaze to prevent it from melting.

Enjoy your **Mazurek**! This Easter cake is a delightful blend of buttery crust, sweet filling, and a touch of festive decoration, making it a cherished part of the holiday celebration.

Sernik Z Owoce (Cheesecake with Fruit)

Ingredients:

For the Crust:

- 1 1/2 cups (150g) graham cracker crumbs or crushed digestive biscuits
- 1/4 cup (50g) granulated sugar
- 1/2 cup (115g) unsalted butter, melted

For the Cheesecake Filling:

- 16 oz (450g) cream cheese, softened
- 1 cup (200g) granulated sugar
- 1 teaspoon vanilla extract
- 3 large eggs
- 1 cup (240ml) sour cream or Greek yogurt
- 1/2 cup (120ml) heavy cream

For the Fruit Topping:

- 2 cups (300g) fresh or frozen fruit (such as berries, peaches, or apricots)
- 1/4 cup (50g) granulated sugar
- 1 tablespoon lemon juice
- 1 tablespoon cornstarch mixed with 2 tablespoons water (optional, for thickening)

Optional Garnish:

- Fresh mint leaves
- Additional fruit for decoration

Instructions:

1. **Prepare the Crust:**
    - Preheat your oven to 350°F (175°C). Grease a 9-inch (23cm) springform pan or line it with parchment paper.
    - In a medium bowl, mix the graham cracker crumbs, granulated sugar, and melted butter until well combined.
    - Press the mixture firmly into the bottom of the prepared pan to form an even layer.
    - Bake in the preheated oven for 10 minutes, then remove from the oven and let cool while preparing the filling.
2. **Prepare the Cheesecake Filling:**
    - In a large bowl, beat the cream cheese until smooth and creamy.
    - Add the granulated sugar and vanilla extract, and mix until well combined.

- Add the eggs one at a time, beating well after each addition.
- Mix in the sour cream (or Greek yogurt) and heavy cream until the mixture is smooth and well combined.

3. **Bake the Cheesecake:**
   - Pour the cream cheese mixture over the cooled crust in the springform pan.
   - Bake in the preheated oven for 55-65 minutes, or until the center is set and the edges are lightly golden.
   - Turn off the oven and crack the oven door slightly. Let the cheesecake cool in the oven for 1 hour.
   - Remove the cheesecake from the oven and refrigerate for at least 4 hours, or preferably overnight, to allow it to set.

4. **Prepare the Fruit Topping:**
   - In a saucepan, combine the fruit, granulated sugar, and lemon juice. Cook over medium heat until the fruit is softened and the mixture is slightly thickened, about 5-7 minutes.
   - If you prefer a thicker sauce, stir in the cornstarch mixture and cook for an additional 1-2 minutes until thickened.
   - Let the fruit topping cool to room temperature.

5. **Assemble and Serve:**
   - Once the cheesecake is fully chilled, spread the cooled fruit topping evenly over the top.
   - Garnish with fresh mint leaves and additional fruit if desired.

6. **Slice and Enjoy:**
   - Slice and serve chilled. The cheesecake can be stored in the refrigerator for up to 5 days.

Tips:

- You can use a variety of fruits depending on what's in season or your personal preference. Berries, peaches, or a mix of fruits work particularly well.
- For a smoother fruit topping, you can blend the fruit before cooking or use a fruit compote.
- To ensure the cheesecake doesn't crack, avoid overmixing the filling and bake it in a water bath if you prefer.

Enjoy your **Sernik Z Owoce**! This cheesecake is a delightful blend of creamy filling and fresh fruit, making it a perfect dessert for any occasion.

Kruszonka (Crumb Topping)

Ingredients:

- 1 cup (125g) all-purpose flour
- 1/2 cup (100g) granulated sugar
- 1/2 cup (115g) unsalted butter, cold and cut into small pieces
- 1/2 teaspoon ground cinnamon (optional, for extra flavor)

Instructions:

1. **Prepare the Ingredients:**
   - Make sure the butter is cold. This helps in creating a crumbly texture for the topping.
2. **Mix the Crumb Topping:**
   - In a medium bowl, combine the flour and sugar. If using cinnamon, add it to the mixture.
   - Add the cold butter pieces to the bowl.
3. **Create the Crumbs:**
   - Use a pastry cutter, two forks, or your fingers to cut the butter into the flour and sugar mixture. Continue until the mixture resembles coarse crumbs with pea-sized pieces of butter throughout.
4. **Use or Store:**
   - Sprinkle the Kruszonka evenly over your cake, pie, or other baked goods before baking.
   - If not using immediately, you can store the crumb topping in an airtight container in the refrigerator for up to a week or freeze it for up to three months.

Tips:

- For a richer flavor, you can use brown sugar instead of granulated sugar or add a pinch of salt.
- To make the topping more aromatic, consider adding a touch of vanilla extract or finely chopped nuts.
- If you prefer a crunchier topping, you can increase the amount of butter or use less flour.

Enjoy your **Kruszonka**! This crumb topping is perfect for adding a sweet, buttery crunch to your favorite baked treats.

Kogel Mogel (Egg Yolk Dessert)

Ingredients:

- 4 large egg yolks
- 1/2 cup (100g) granulated sugar
- 1 teaspoon vanilla extract (optional)
- 1 tablespoon cocoa powder (optional, for chocolate flavor)
- A pinch of ground cinnamon (optional, for added flavor)

Instructions:

1. **Prepare the Ingredients:**
   - Ensure the egg yolks are at room temperature for better consistency.
2. **Mix the Egg Yolks and Sugar:**
   - In a medium bowl, whisk the egg yolks and granulated sugar together until the mixture is smooth and slightly thickened. This can be done with a hand whisk or an electric mixer. The sugar should be fully dissolved, and the mixture should become creamy and pale.
3. **Add Flavorings (Optional):**
   - If you like, add vanilla extract to the mixture for a subtle vanilla flavor.
   - For a chocolate twist, sift in the cocoa powder and mix until well combined.
   - You can also add a pinch of ground cinnamon for a warm, spicy note.
4. **Serve:**
   - Spoon the Kogel Mogel into serving bowls or glasses.
   - Chill in the refrigerator for at least 30 minutes before serving if you prefer it cold, or serve immediately at room temperature.
5. **Garnish (Optional):**
   - You can garnish with a sprinkle of cinnamon, a dollop of whipped cream, or fresh fruit if desired.

Tips:

- Ensure the egg yolks are fresh and from a reliable source, as this dessert is not cooked.
- For added texture, you can mix in some crushed cookies or a small handful of nuts before serving.
- This dessert can be customized with other flavorings such as almond extract or a bit of citrus zest.

Kogel Mogel is a rich and nostalgic treat that highlights the simplicity and deliciousness of basic ingredients. Enjoy this comforting dessert as a sweet end to your meal!

Śliwki w Czekoladzie (Plums in Chocolate)

Ingredients:

- 1 cup (200g) dried plums (prunes), pitted
- 6 oz (170g) dark chocolate (70% cocoa or your preference), chopped
- 2 tablespoons unsalted butter or coconut oil (optional, for smoother chocolate coating)
- Sea salt (optional, for garnish)
- Chopped nuts or shredded coconut (optional, for garnish)

Instructions:

1. **Prepare the Dried Plums:**
    - Ensure the dried plums are pitted. If they are slightly tough or dry, you can soak them in warm water for about 10 minutes to soften them. Drain and pat them dry with paper towels.
2. **Melt the Chocolate:**
    - In a heatproof bowl, melt the dark chocolate using a double boiler or microwave. To use the double boiler method, place the bowl over a pot of simmering water, making sure the bowl doesn't touch the water. Stir until the chocolate is completely melted.
    - If using the microwave, heat the chocolate in 30-second intervals, stirring after each interval until fully melted.
    - For a smoother coating, you can stir in the butter or coconut oil into the melted chocolate.
3. **Coat the Plums:**
    - Dip each dried plum into the melted chocolate, using a fork or skewer to hold it and ensure it's fully coated.
    - Let any excess chocolate drip off.
4. **Set the Chocolate:**
    - Place the chocolate-coated plums on a parchment-lined baking sheet.
    - If desired, sprinkle a small pinch of sea salt on top of each plum for a touch of contrast.
    - Optionally, you can also sprinkle chopped nuts or shredded coconut on top before the chocolate sets.
5. **Chill and Serve:**
    - Refrigerate the plums until the chocolate is fully set, about 30 minutes.
    - Store the chocolate-covered plums in an airtight container in the refrigerator for up to 2 weeks.

Tips:

- You can use milk chocolate or white chocolate if you prefer a sweeter coating.

- For added flavor, consider adding a splash of liqueur (such as brandy or orange liqueur) to the melted chocolate.
- If you want to make these for a special occasion, you can also drizzle a different type of chocolate over the set plums for an elegant touch.

Enjoy your **Śliwki w Czekoladzie**! These chocolate-covered plums are a delicious and sophisticated treat that combines the natural sweetness and tartness of the fruit with rich, creamy chocolate.

Rogaliki Świętomarcińskie (St. Martin's Croissants)

Ingredients:

For the Dough:

- 3 1/2 cups (450g) all-purpose flour
- 1 cup (240ml) milk, warm
- 1/2 cup (115g) unsalted butter, softened
- 1/4 cup (50g) granulated sugar
- 2 large eggs
- 2 teaspoons active dry yeast
- 1/2 teaspoon salt

For the Poppy Seed Filling:

- 1 cup (150g) poppy seeds
- 1 cup (200g) granulated sugar
- 1/2 cup (120ml) milk
- 1/4 cup (60g) unsalted butter
- 1/4 cup (60ml) honey
- 1 teaspoon vanilla extract
- 1/4 cup (30g) chopped nuts (optional)
- 1/4 cup (50g) raisins (optional)

For the Glaze:

- 1 egg, beaten
- Powdered sugar (optional, for dusting)

Instructions:

1. **Prepare the Dough:**
   - In a small bowl, dissolve the yeast in warm milk and let it sit for about 5 minutes until it becomes frothy.
   - In a large bowl, mix the flour, sugar, and salt. Make a well in the center and add the yeast mixture, softened butter, and eggs.
   - Knead the dough until it is smooth and elastic, about 5-7 minutes. You can do this by hand or with a stand mixer fitted with a dough hook.
   - Place the dough in a lightly greased bowl, cover it with a cloth, and let it rise in a warm place for about 1-2 hours or until it has doubled in size.
2. **Prepare the Poppy Seed Filling:**
   - In a saucepan, combine the poppy seeds, sugar, milk, butter, and honey. Cook over medium heat, stirring frequently, until the mixture thickens and becomes paste-like, about 5-7 minutes.

- Remove from heat and stir in the vanilla extract. If using, mix in the chopped nuts and raisins. Allow the filling to cool.

3. **Assemble the Croissants:**
   - Preheat your oven to 375°F (190°C) and line a baking sheet with parchment paper.
   - Punch down the risen dough and divide it into two portions. Roll each portion into a circle about 1/4 inch (6mm) thick.
   - Spread a thin layer of the poppy seed filling over each dough circle.
   - Cut each circle into wedges (like slicing a pizza) and roll each wedge from the wide end to the tip to form a crescent shape.
   - Place the rolled croissants on the prepared baking sheet.

4. **Glaze and Bake:**
   - Brush the croissants with the beaten egg to give them a golden finish.
   - Bake in the preheated oven for 15-20 minutes, or until they are golden brown and puffed up.
   - Remove from the oven and let them cool on a wire rack.

5. **Finish and Serve:**
   - If desired, dust the cooled croissants with powdered sugar before serving.

Tips:

- Make sure the filling is well-cooked and cooled before spreading it on the dough to avoid sogginess.
- You can adjust the sweetness of the filling to your taste by modifying the amount of sugar or honey.
- These croissants can be enjoyed fresh or stored in an airtight container for a few days.

Enjoy your **Rogaliki Świętomarcińskie**! These sweet, poppy-seed-filled pastries are perfect for celebrating St. Martin's Day or simply enjoying a delicious treat with your tea or coffee.

Tarta Rabarbarowa (Rhubarb Tart)

Ingredients:

For the Crust:

- 1 1/2 cups (190g) all-purpose flour
- 1/2 cup (100g) granulated sugar
- 1/2 teaspoon baking powder
- 1/4 teaspoon salt
- 1/2 cup (115g) unsalted butter, cold and cut into small pieces
- 1 large egg yolk
- 2-3 tablespoons cold water

For the Rhubarb Filling:

- 4 cups (400g) fresh rhubarb, chopped into 1/2-inch pieces
- 1 cup (200g) granulated sugar
- 1/4 cup (30g) all-purpose flour
- 1/4 teaspoon ground cinnamon (optional)
- 1 tablespoon lemon juice

For the Cream Filling (Optional):

- 1 cup (240ml) heavy cream
- 1/2 cup (100g) granulated sugar
- 1 teaspoon vanilla extract
- 1 tablespoon all-purpose flour

Instructions:

1. **Prepare the Crust:**
    - Preheat your oven to 375°F (190°C). Grease or line a 9-inch (23cm) tart pan with parchment paper.
    - In a large bowl, whisk together the flour, granulated sugar, baking powder, and salt.
    - Cut in the cold butter using a pastry cutter or your fingers until the mixture resembles coarse crumbs.
    - Add the egg yolk and mix until combined. Gradually add cold water, one tablespoon at a time, until the dough comes together.
    - Form the dough into a disk, wrap it in plastic wrap, and refrigerate for at least 30 minutes.
2. **Pre-bake the Crust:**
    - Roll out the chilled dough on a lightly floured surface to fit the tart pan.

- Transfer the dough to the pan, pressing it into the bottom and up the sides. Trim any excess dough.
- Prick the bottom of the crust with a fork to prevent bubbling.
- Bake in the preheated oven for 10 minutes, then remove and let it cool slightly.

3. **Prepare the Rhubarb Filling:**
   - In a large bowl, combine the chopped rhubarb, granulated sugar, flour, cinnamon (if using), and lemon juice. Toss to coat the rhubarb evenly.

4. **Assemble the Tart:**
   - If using the cream filling, whip the heavy cream with granulated sugar and vanilla extract until soft peaks form. Stir in the flour.
   - Spread the cream filling evenly over the pre-baked crust if using.
   - Spoon the rhubarb mixture on top of the cream filling or directly onto the crust if not using cream.

5. **Bake the Tart:**
   - Return the tart to the oven and bake for 30-35 minutes, or until the rhubarb is tender and the crust is golden brown. If the tart starts to brown too quickly, cover the edges with aluminum foil.

6. **Cool and Serve:**
   - Allow the tart to cool completely before serving. This allows the filling to set properly.

Tips:

- Rhubarb is quite tart, so you can adjust the amount of sugar in the filling to suit your taste.
- For a slightly sweeter or more complex flavor, you can add a touch of vanilla extract or almond extract to the filling.
- If you prefer a more rustic tart, you can fold the edges of the dough over the filling to create a free-form galette instead of using a tart pan.

Enjoy your **Tarta Rabarbarowa**! This tart is a wonderful way to enjoy the unique tartness of rhubarb with a buttery crust and, optionally, a creamy layer that complements the fruit beautifully.

Ciasto Malinowe (Raspberry Cake)

Ingredients:

For the Sponge Cake:

- 1 cup (125g) all-purpose flour
- 1 cup (200g) granulated sugar
- 1/2 cup (120ml) vegetable oil
- 1/2 cup (120ml) milk
- 3 large eggs
- 1 teaspoon vanilla extract
- 1 1/2 teaspoons baking powder
- 1/4 teaspoon salt

For the Raspberry Filling:

- 2 cups (300g) fresh or frozen raspberries
- 1/2 cup (100g) granulated sugar
- 1 tablespoon lemon juice
- 1 tablespoon cornstarch mixed with 2 tablespoons water

For the Cream Topping:

- 1 cup (240ml) heavy cream
- 1/4 cup (50g) granulated sugar
- 1 teaspoon vanilla extract
- Fresh raspberries for garnish

Instructions:

1. **Prepare the Sponge Cake:**
    - Preheat your oven to 350°F (175°C). Grease and flour an 8-inch (20cm) round cake pan or line it with parchment paper.
    - In a large bowl, whisk together the flour, sugar, baking powder, and salt.
    - In another bowl, combine the eggs, vegetable oil, milk, and vanilla extract. Beat until well mixed.
    - Gradually add the wet ingredients to the dry ingredients, mixing until just combined.
    - Pour the batter into the prepared cake pan and smooth the top with a spatula.
    - Bake for 25-30 minutes, or until a toothpick inserted into the center comes out clean. Let the cake cool in the pan for 10 minutes, then transfer it to a wire rack to cool completely.
2. **Prepare the Raspberry Filling:**

- In a medium saucepan, combine the raspberries, granulated sugar, and lemon juice. Cook over medium heat, stirring occasionally, until the raspberries break down and the mixture starts to thicken, about 5-7 minutes.
- Stir in the cornstarch mixture and cook for an additional 1-2 minutes until the filling is thick and glossy. Remove from heat and let it cool.

3. **Prepare the Cream Topping:**
   - In a large bowl, whip the heavy cream with granulated sugar and vanilla extract until stiff peaks form.
4. **Assemble the Cake:**
   - Once the cake has completely cooled, slice it horizontally into two layers.
   - Spread the raspberry filling evenly over the bottom layer of the cake.
   - Place the top layer of the cake on top of the raspberry filling.
   - Spread the whipped cream topping evenly over the top and sides of the cake.
   - Garnish with fresh raspberries.
5. **Chill and Serve:**
   - Refrigerate the cake for at least 1 hour before serving to allow the flavors to meld and the topping to set.

Tips:

- For a more intense raspberry flavor, you can add a bit of raspberry extract to the cream topping.
- If fresh raspberries are not available, you can use frozen raspberries. Just make sure to thaw and drain them before using.
- This cake can be made a day ahead; just keep it refrigerated until you're ready to serve.

Enjoy your **Ciasto Malinowe**! This raspberry cake is a light, fruity, and refreshing dessert that's sure to impress with its vibrant color and delicious flavor.

Czernina (Duck Blood Soup with Raisins)

Ingredients:

For the Duck Stock:

- 1 whole duck (about 4-5 pounds), cleaned and cut into pieces
- 1 onion, peeled and halved
- 2 carrots, peeled and cut into chunks
- 1 parsnip, peeled and cut into chunks
- 2 stalks celery, cut into chunks
- 3-4 cloves garlic, peeled
- 2 bay leaves
- 10-12 whole black peppercorns
- Salt, to taste
- Water, enough to cover the duck (about 8 cups)

For the Soup:

- 1 cup (240ml) duck blood (from a butcher or specialty store)
- 1 cup (150g) raisins
- 1-2 tablespoons vinegar (white or apple cider)
- 1 apple, peeled, cored, and diced (optional)
- 1 tablespoon sugar (adjust to taste)
- Salt and black pepper, to taste
- 1 tablespoon vegetable oil or duck fat
- Fresh dill or parsley, for garnish

Instructions:

1. **Prepare the Duck Stock:**
   - In a large pot, place the duck pieces and cover them with water. Bring to a boil over high heat. Skim off any foam that rises to the surface.
   - Add the onion, carrots, parsnip, celery, garlic, bay leaves, peppercorns, and salt to the pot.
   - Reduce the heat to low and simmer for about 1.5 to 2 hours, or until the duck is tender.
   - Remove the duck pieces and strain the stock to remove the vegetables and spices. Set the stock aside.
2. **Prepare the Soup:**
   - In a separate pot, heat the vegetable oil or duck fat over medium heat.
   - If using, sauté the diced apple until soft and slightly caramelized.
   - Add the strained duck stock to the pot with the apples (if using).
   - Stir in the raisins and bring the mixture to a gentle simmer.
   - Mix the duck blood with a small amount of the hot stock to temper it (this prevents it from curdling). Gradually stir the tempered blood into the soup.

- Simmer the soup gently for about 10 minutes. Do not boil after adding the blood, as this can cause it to curdle.
            - Add vinegar and sugar to balance the flavors. Adjust the seasoning with salt and pepper to taste.
    3. **Serve:**
        - Ladle the soup into bowls and garnish with fresh dill or parsley.

Tips:

- If you cannot find duck blood, you can substitute it with pig's blood, but the flavor will be slightly different.
- The soup can be made a day in advance and stored in the refrigerator. The flavors often improve after a day.
- Some variations of Czernina include adding sliced cooked duck meat back into the soup for added substance.

Czernina is a unique and flavorful dish that reflects the rich culinary traditions of Poland. Enjoy this classic soup with its distinctive taste and hearty character!

Placek Z Cynamonem (Cinnamon Cake)

Ingredients:

For the Cake:

- 2 cups (250g) all-purpose flour
- 1 cup (200g) granulated sugar
- 1/2 cup (115g) unsalted butter, softened
- 1/2 cup (120ml) milk
- 3 large eggs
- 1 tablespoon baking powder
- 1 teaspoon vanilla extract
- 1/4 teaspoon salt

For the Cinnamon Swirl:

- 1/4 cup (50g) granulated sugar
- 2 tablespoons ground cinnamon
- 1 tablespoon unsalted butter, melted

For the Topping (Optional):

- Powdered sugar, for dusting

Instructions:

1. **Preheat the Oven:**
   - Preheat your oven to 350°F (175°C). Grease and flour a 9-inch (23cm) round cake pan or line it with parchment paper.
2. **Prepare the Cake Batter:**
   - In a large bowl, cream together the softened butter and granulated sugar until light and fluffy.
   - Add the eggs one at a time, beating well after each addition.
   - Mix in the vanilla extract.
   - In a separate bowl, whisk together the flour, baking powder, and salt.
   - Gradually add the dry ingredients to the butter mixture, alternating with the milk, beginning and ending with the flour mixture. Mix until just combined.
3. **Prepare the Cinnamon Swirl:**
   - In a small bowl, combine the granulated sugar and ground cinnamon.
   - Stir in the melted butter until the mixture forms a crumbly texture.
4. **Assemble the Cake:**
   - Pour half of the cake batter into the prepared cake pan.
   - Sprinkle half of the cinnamon swirl mixture evenly over the batter.

- Top with the remaining batter and then sprinkle the remaining cinnamon swirl mixture on top.
5. **Swirl the Cinnamon Mixture:**
   - Use a knife or skewer to gently swirl the cinnamon mixture into the batter, creating a marble effect. Do not overmix.
6. **Bake the Cake:**
   - Bake in the preheated oven for 30-35 minutes, or until a toothpick inserted into the center comes out clean.
   - Allow the cake to cool in the pan for about 10 minutes, then transfer it to a wire rack to cool completely.
7. **Serve:**
   - If desired, dust the cooled cake with powdered sugar before serving.

Tips:

- For a richer flavor, you can use brown sugar in the cinnamon swirl mixture.
- You can also add chopped nuts, such as walnuts or pecans, to the cinnamon swirl mixture for added texture.
- To make the cake more indulgent, you can drizzle a simple glaze made from powdered sugar and milk over the cooled cake.

Enjoy your **Placek z Cynamonem**! This easy-to-make cinnamon cake is sure to fill your kitchen with a warm, inviting aroma and provides a deliciously comforting treat for any time of day.

Ciasto Dyniowe (Pumpkin Cake)

Ingredients:

For the Cake:

- 1 1/2 cups (190g) all-purpose flour
- 1 cup (200g) granulated sugar
- 1/2 cup (115g) unsalted butter, softened
- 1 cup (240ml) canned pumpkin puree (not pumpkin pie filling)
- 3 large eggs
- 1/2 cup (120ml) vegetable oil
- 1 teaspoon vanilla extract
- 1 teaspoon ground cinnamon
- 1/2 teaspoon ground ginger
- 1/4 teaspoon ground nutmeg
- 1/4 teaspoon ground cloves
- 1/2 teaspoon baking powder
- 1/2 teaspoon baking soda
- 1/4 teaspoon salt

For the Cream Cheese Frosting:

- 1/2 cup (115g) unsalted butter, softened
- 8 oz (225g) cream cheese, softened
- 3 cups (360g) powdered sugar
- 1 teaspoon vanilla extract

Instructions:

1. **Prepare the Cake:**
    - Preheat your oven to 350°F (175°C). Grease and flour a 9-inch (23cm) round cake pan or line it with parchment paper. You can also use a 9x13-inch (23x33cm) baking dish if you prefer a sheet cake.
    - In a medium bowl, whisk together the flour, baking powder, baking soda, salt, and spices (cinnamon, ginger, nutmeg, cloves).
    - In a large bowl, beat the softened butter and granulated sugar together until light and fluffy.
    - Add the eggs one at a time, beating well after each addition.
    - Mix in the pumpkin puree and vanilla extract.
    - Gradually add the dry ingredients to the wet ingredients, alternating with the vegetable oil, beginning and ending with the dry ingredients. Mix until just combined.
    - Pour the batter into the prepared pan and smooth the top with a spatula.

2. **Bake the Cake:**
   - Bake in the preheated oven for 30-35 minutes (for a round pan) or 25-30 minutes (for a sheet pan), or until a toothpick inserted into the center comes out clean.
   - Let the cake cool in the pan for about 10 minutes, then transfer it to a wire rack to cool completely.
3. **Prepare the Cream Cheese Frosting:**
   - In a large bowl, beat the softened butter and cream cheese together until smooth and creamy.
   - Gradually add the powdered sugar, beating well after each addition.
   - Mix in the vanilla extract.
   - Beat until the frosting is light and fluffy.
4. **Frost the Cake:**
   - Once the cake is completely cooled, spread the cream cheese frosting evenly over the top and sides of the cake.
   - You can also add a sprinkle of cinnamon or a few chopped nuts for garnish, if desired.
5. **Serve:**
   - Slice and serve the cake. It's perfect with a cup of coffee or tea!

Tips:

- For added texture, consider mixing in some chopped nuts or chocolate chips into the batter.
- If you prefer a lighter cake, you can use half the amount of oil and replace it with unsweetened applesauce.
- To ensure a moist cake, be careful not to overmix the batter.

Enjoy your **Ciasto Dyniowe**! This pumpkin cake is a cozy and flavorful treat that highlights the rich, earthy taste of pumpkin, complemented by a creamy and tangy cream cheese frosting.

Zupa Jabłkowa (Apple Soup)

Ingredients:

For the Soup:

- 4 medium apples (such as Granny Smith or any tart apple), peeled, cored, and chopped
- 1 medium onion, peeled and chopped
- 1 carrot, peeled and chopped
- 1 stalk celery, chopped
- 4 cups (1 liter) chicken or vegetable broth
- 1 tablespoon butter or vegetable oil
- 1-2 tablespoons granulated sugar (adjust to taste)
- 1/2 teaspoon ground cinnamon
- 1/4 teaspoon ground nutmeg
- 1 tablespoon lemon juice
- Salt and black pepper, to taste

For Garnish (Optional):

- Fresh cream or sour cream
- Chopped fresh herbs (such as parsley or dill)
- Croutons or toasted bread

Instructions:

1. **Prepare the Ingredients:**
   - Peel, core, and chop the apples. Set aside.
   - Chop the onion, carrot, and celery.
2. **Cook the Vegetables:**
   - In a large pot, heat the butter or vegetable oil over medium heat.
   - Add the chopped onion, carrot, and celery. Cook, stirring occasionally, until the vegetables are softened, about 5-7 minutes.
3. **Add the Apples:**
   - Add the chopped apples to the pot and cook for an additional 5 minutes, allowing the apples to soften and meld with the vegetables.
4. **Simmer the Soup:**
   - Pour the chicken or vegetable broth into the pot and bring to a boil.
   - Reduce the heat to low and simmer for about 20 minutes, or until the apples and vegetables are tender.
5. **Blend the Soup:**
   - Using an immersion blender, blend the soup until smooth. If you don't have an immersion blender, you can carefully transfer the soup in batches to a blender and blend until smooth. Be cautious with hot liquids.

6. **Season the Soup:**
   - Return the soup to the pot if you used a blender. Stir in the sugar, cinnamon, nutmeg, and lemon juice. Adjust the seasoning with salt and black pepper to taste.
   - Simmer for an additional 5 minutes to allow the flavors to meld.
7. **Serve:**
   - Ladle the soup into bowls and garnish with a dollop of fresh cream or sour cream if desired.
   - Sprinkle with chopped fresh herbs and add croutons or toasted bread for added texture.

Tips:

- The choice of apples can affect the sweetness and tartness of the soup. Adjust the amount of sugar according to your taste and the type of apples used.
- For a more complex flavor, consider adding a splash of white wine or a hint of curry powder.
- If you prefer a chunkier texture, you can blend only half of the soup and leave the rest with chunks of apples and vegetables.

Enjoy your **Zupa Jabłkowa**! This unique and comforting apple soup is a wonderful way to enjoy apples in a savory dish, offering a delightful combination of sweet and savory flavors.

Pączki z Różą (Rose-filled Doughnuts)

Ingredients:

For the Doughnuts:

- 3 1/2 cups (440g) all-purpose flour
- 1/2 cup (100g) granulated sugar
- 1/2 cup (120ml) whole milk, warmed
- 1/4 cup (60g) unsalted butter, softened
- 3 large eggs
- 1/4 cup (60ml) water
- 2 teaspoons active dry yeast
- 1/2 teaspoon salt
- 1 teaspoon vanilla extract
- 1 tablespoon rum or brandy (optional)
- Vegetable oil, for frying

For the Rose Filling:

- 1/2 cup (150g) rose jam or rose preserve
- 1/4 cup (60ml) water
- 1 tablespoon cornstarch

For the Glaze:

- 1 cup (120g) powdered sugar
- 2-3 tablespoons milk
- 1/2 teaspoon vanilla extract

For Garnish (Optional):

- Finely chopped pistachios
- Edible rose petals

Instructions:

1. **Prepare the Dough:**
    - In a small bowl, dissolve the active dry yeast in the warm milk with a pinch of sugar. Let it sit for about 5-10 minutes until frothy.
    - In a large bowl, combine the flour and granulated sugar. Create a well in the center.
    - Add the yeast mixture, softened butter, eggs, vanilla extract, and rum (if using) to the well.

- Mix until a sticky dough forms. Knead the dough on a floured surface or using a stand mixer with a dough hook for about 5-7 minutes, until smooth and elastic.
- Place the dough in a greased bowl, cover it with a damp cloth or plastic wrap, and let it rise in a warm place for about 1-1.5 hours, or until doubled in size.

2. **Prepare the Rose Filling:**
   - In a small saucepan, combine the rose jam and water. Heat gently until the jam melts and becomes liquid.
   - Dissolve the cornstarch in a small amount of water and stir into the rose jam mixture. Cook, stirring constantly, until the filling thickens. Let it cool.

3. **Shape and Fry the Doughnuts:**
   - Once the dough has risen, punch it down and turn it out onto a floured surface. Roll it out to about 1/2-inch (1.25 cm) thickness.
   - Use a round cutter (about 2-3 inches in diameter) to cut out dough rounds. Gather and re-roll any scraps.
   - Place a small spoonful of rose filling in the center of half of the dough rounds. Brush the edges with a little water, then top with another dough round, pressing the edges to seal.
   - Let the filled doughnuts rise on a floured surface for another 30 minutes.

4. **Fry the Doughnuts:**
   - Heat vegetable oil in a deep fryer or large pot to 350°F (175°C).
   - Fry the doughnuts in batches, being careful not to overcrowd the pot. Fry for about 2-3 minutes per side, or until golden brown.
   - Remove with a slotted spoon and drain on paper towels.

5. **Prepare the Glaze:**
   - In a medium bowl, whisk together the powdered sugar, milk, and vanilla extract until smooth.

6. **Glaze the Doughnuts:**
   - While the doughnuts are still warm, dip them into the glaze, coating them evenly. Allow any excess glaze to drip off.

7. **Garnish (Optional):**
   - Before the glaze sets, you can sprinkle the doughnuts with finely chopped pistachios or edible rose petals for a decorative touch.

Tips:

- Ensure the oil temperature remains consistent for even frying and to prevent the doughnuts from becoming too greasy.
- If you don't have rose jam, you can use other fruit preserves or a flavored pastry cream as an alternative filling.

Enjoy your **Pączki z Różą**! These rose-filled doughnuts are a delightful treat, combining the rich, sweet flavor of rose with the soft, airy texture of freshly fried doughnuts.

Kardamonowe Bułeczki (Cardamom Buns)

Ingredients:

For the Dough:

- 3 1/2 cups (440g) all-purpose flour
- 1/2 cup (100g) granulated sugar
- 1/2 cup (120ml) milk, warmed
- 1/2 cup (115g) unsalted butter, softened
- 2 large eggs
- 1/4 cup (60ml) water
- 1/4 cup (60ml) sour cream or plain yogurt
- 1 packet (2 1/4 teaspoons) active dry yeast
- 1 teaspoon ground cardamom
- 1/4 teaspoon salt

For the Filling:

- 1/4 cup (50g) unsalted butter, softened
- 1/4 cup (50g) granulated sugar
- 2 tablespoons ground cardamom

For the Egg Wash:

- 1 egg, beaten
- 1 tablespoon water

For Garnish (Optional):

- Pearl sugar or coarse sugar
- Sliced almonds

Instructions:

1. **Prepare the Dough:**
    - In a small bowl, dissolve the active dry yeast in the warmed milk with a pinch of sugar. Let it sit for about 5-10 minutes until frothy.
    - In a large bowl, combine the flour, sugar, ground cardamom, and salt.
    - Make a well in the center and add the yeast mixture, softened butter, eggs, water, and sour cream or yogurt.
    - Mix until a sticky dough forms. Knead the dough on a floured surface or in a stand mixer with a dough hook for about 5-7 minutes, until smooth and elastic.
    - Place the dough in a greased bowl, cover it with a damp cloth or plastic wrap, and let it rise in a warm place for about 1-1.5 hours, or until doubled in size.

2. **Prepare the Filling:**
   - In a small bowl, mix together the softened butter, granulated sugar, and ground cardamom until well combined.
3. **Shape the Buns:**
   - Once the dough has risen, punch it down and turn it out onto a floured surface. Roll it out into a rectangle about 1/4-inch (0.6 cm) thick.
   - Spread the cardamom filling evenly over the dough.
   - Roll the dough up tightly from one long side to form a log.
   - Slice the log into 12-15 even pieces.
   - Place the slices cut side up on a baking sheet lined with parchment paper, spacing them a few inches apart.
4. **Let the Buns Rise:**
   - Cover the shaped buns with a clean cloth and let them rise for about 30 minutes, or until puffy and nearly doubled in size.
5. **Preheat the Oven:**
   - Preheat your oven to 375°F (190°C).
6. **Prepare the Egg Wash:**
   - In a small bowl, whisk together the beaten egg and water.
   - Brush the egg wash over the tops of the buns.
7. **Bake the Buns:**
   - Bake in the preheated oven for 15-20 minutes, or until golden brown.
   - Remove from the oven and let cool slightly on a wire rack.
8. **Garnish (Optional):**
   - Before the buns cool completely, sprinkle with pearl sugar or coarse sugar and sliced almonds if desired.

Tips:

- The cardamom buns can be enjoyed warm or at room temperature. They're best consumed within a day or two, but they can be frozen for later use.
- For an extra touch of flavor, you can add a light glaze made from powdered sugar and milk to the cooled buns.

Enjoy your **Kardamonowe Bułeczki**! These cardamom buns are a wonderfully aromatic and sweet treat that will fill your kitchen with a delightful scent and offer a perfect bite of comfort.

Tarta Cytrynowa (Lemon Tart)

Ingredients:

For the Tart Crust:

- 1 1/2 cups (190g) all-purpose flour
- 1/2 cup (100g) granulated sugar
- 1/2 cup (115g) unsalted butter, cold and cut into small cubes
- 1 large egg yolk
- 1-2 tablespoons cold water (as needed)

For the Lemon Filling:

- 3/4 cup (150g) granulated sugar
- 1/2 cup (120ml) freshly squeezed lemon juice (about 2-3 lemons)
- 1 tablespoon lemon zest
- 3 large eggs
- 1/2 cup (115g) unsalted butter, cut into small cubes

For Garnish (Optional):

- Powdered sugar, for dusting
- Lemon zest or thin lemon slices

Instructions:

1. **Prepare the Tart Crust:**
    - In a food processor, combine the flour and granulated sugar.
    - Add the cold butter and pulse until the mixture resembles coarse crumbs.
    - Add the egg yolk and pulse until just combined.
    - If the dough is too dry, add cold water, one tablespoon at a time, until the dough comes together.
    - Turn the dough out onto a lightly floured surface and shape it into a disk. Wrap in plastic wrap and refrigerate for at least 30 minutes.
2. **Preheat the Oven:**
    - Preheat your oven to 375°F (190°C).
3. **Roll Out the Dough:**
    - On a lightly floured surface, roll out the chilled dough to about 1/8-inch (3mm) thickness.
    - Carefully transfer the dough to a 9-inch (23cm) tart pan with a removable bottom. Press the dough into the pan and trim the edges.
    - Prick the bottom of the tart shell with a fork to prevent bubbling.
4. **Blind Bake the Crust:**
    - Line the tart shell with parchment paper and fill with pie weights or dried beans.

- Bake in the preheated oven for 15 minutes.
- Remove the parchment paper and weights, then bake for an additional 5 minutes, or until the crust is lightly golden. Let it cool completely.

5. **Prepare the Lemon Filling:**
    - In a medium saucepan, whisk together the granulated sugar, lemon juice, and lemon zest.
    - Add the eggs and whisk until well combined.
    - Place the saucepan over medium heat and cook, stirring constantly, until the mixture thickens and reaches 170°F (77°C) on a thermometer. Do not let it boil.
    - Remove from heat and stir in the butter until melted and smooth.
6. **Fill the Tart:**
    - Pour the lemon filling into the cooled tart crust.
    - Smooth the top with a spatula.
7. **Bake the Tart:**
    - Bake in the preheated oven for 15-20 minutes, or until the filling is set and the surface is just starting to brown slightly.
    - Allow the tart to cool to room temperature, then refrigerate for at least 2 hours to set completely.
8. **Garnish and Serve:**
    - Before serving, dust the top of the tart with powdered sugar and garnish with additional lemon zest or thin lemon slices if desired.

Tips:

- To ensure a smooth filling, strain the lemon mixture through a fine mesh sieve before pouring it into the tart crust.
- The tart can be made a day in advance and stored in the refrigerator. It keeps well for up to 3 days.

Enjoy your **Tarta Cytrynowa**! This lemon tart is a perfect balance of tangy and sweet, with a crisp, buttery crust that complements the bright lemon filling.

www.ingramcontent.com/pod-product-compliance
Lightning Source LLC
LaVergne TN
LVHW081555060526
838201LV00054B/1897